This book is addressing a very important issue in the body of Christ, the institution of marriage and the role of fathers. Once again, God is bringing to our remembrance His original intent for the procreation of the human race. God's original pattern and design remain the same, even though man has become humanistic in his thinking and continually tries to reinvent God's formula. God has not changed His character, His intentions, or His will concerning marriage. It is still a divine institution. Even though God made a way through the death of His Son for man's deliverance and the reconciliation of the relationship between God and man, the process of sanctification and restoration takes time, primarily because of the hardness of man's heart and his inherent selfish and rebellious nature. The author gives valuable revelation and insights that any true believer can relate to. The foundations and the old landmarks must not be removed; they must be maintained, for they are the pattern for the new generation of sons of God and the expressions of God's heart. I highly recommend this book.

—Apostle John E. Wilson
St. John's Full Gospel Deliverance Church
Bloomfield, Connecticut

THE
PURPOSE FOR
MARRIAGE

THE
PURPOSE FOR
MARRIAGE

GEMMA VALENTINE

CREATION HOUSE
A STRANG COMPANY

The Purpose for Marriage by Gemma Valentine
Published by Creation House
A Strang Company
600 Rinehart Road
Lake Mary, Florida 32746
www.creationhouse.com

Design Director: Bill Johnson
Cover Designer: Amanda Potter

Library of Congress Control Number: 2008941345
International Standard Book Number: 978-1-59979-601-7

First Edition

08 09 10 11 12 — 9 8 7 6 5 4 3 2 1
Printed in the United States of America

This book is dedicated to Pastor George Irabor and the members of Fountain of Grace Church located in Dedham, Massachusetts. Thank you for your unbridled passion toward God's institution of marriage and the family. I also thank my husband for his input, love, and support. Many of the insights in this book came from a lifetime of experience.

CONTENTS

FOREWORD

THERE ARE MANY VOICES IN THIS WORLD, AND EACH VOICE IS SEEKING expression in different ways. The author of this book is using this medium of expression to convey the thoughts, heart, and mind of God concerning this very important topic. When God's original intent for man gets out of alignment, God looks at the blueprints, which are the original design, and He begins to stir up the pure minds of His people concerning His position on any given topic.

Each chapter in this book answers the relevant questions of today concerning marriage and the role of fathers. These subjects bring clarity and understanding of many underlying issues facing the Christian community and today's generation. The purpose of marriage must be defined for this generation of children, who for the most part have grown up without fathers. Each succeeding generation has to be informed so that order can be established and distinct boundaries can be reset. This responsibility has been given to the fathers of the preceding generation. Their failure will result in their children living their lives contrary to the principles set by God.

The revelations, scriptural references, and general information in this book will enlighten, instruct, deliver, restore, inform, and bring needed understanding to the church on every level. Once again, the voice of the Lord is sounding forth a word of correction, edification, and exhortation of these vital truths to this generation in the body of Christ, and it will profit us if we would take heed.

—BISHOP MERVIN JORDAN
GOING PLACES WITH JESUS MINISTRY
FORT LAUDERDALE, FLORIDA

ACKNOWLEDGMENTS

MY HUSBAND AND I MOVED TO TEXAS IN OCTOBER OF 2005. AT THE beginning of 2006, certain prophets were searching for us with a word from the Lord. The word was that the time had come for me to walk in another dimension of the Spirit—that God was elevating me in my calling. Anytime God elevates a person, He places someone in his or her life to give them counsel and instructions.

The ministry God connected me with was Bill Smith Ministries (www. drbillsmith.org). I met Dr. Bill and Nadine Smith at Christ as Life Church on my arrival in Texas eighteen months before they went into semi-retirement. Dr. Bill Smith is an apostle who has been in ministry for over fifty years. Their work in missions includes the establishing of the kingdom of God in many nations in Africa, Europe, India, and the Americas. They have impacted the lives of thousands of people, raising sons and daughters in the ministry, prophesying to rulers of nations, and functioning as the apostolic covering over many churches in various parts of the world. Their radio ministry reaches many nations throughout the world including Africa, Northern Ireland, the Pacific Rim, Europe, and America. Even though they are no longer pastoring, Dr. Bill continues to teach ministers at his mentoring classes in Anna, Texas. He has a wealth of knowledge, wisdom, and revelation of the Word. The glory and anointing resting on his life was imparted through visitations from the Lord—who taught him much of what he continues to impart to others at his mentoring classes.

I thank God for the tutelage of Dr. Bill Smith. I am excited to know that the knowledge I have gained is not from the mistakes of youthful service but from a mature life that is rooted and grounded in a relationship with God, and years of wisdom gained by experience and a life of walking in the supernatural.

Thank you, Apostle Bill.

Prophetic Word From Apostle Bill Smith

For the Lord God says unto you, "I have called you, and I have raised you up, and I have given you the ability to write; therefore, you will understand that the books that you write will be used, for I have called you to make people understand the ways of the Lord. You shall write simple, so they will understand, but you shall write the truth, and I, the Lord God, will impart it to their hearts as you write, and you will find that the doors will open to more than Trinidad because there will be a calling from the east, west, north, and south from this day forward. Your ministry will expand, even as you have planned," says the Lord. "And the healing ministry and miraculous ministry will flow before you. Always create an open door. Therefore, finances will not be a problem for you as you obey Me, and you will find that your husband will move into the ministry with you." Amen.

INTRODUCTION

Let us rejoice and shout for joy [exulting and triumphant]!
Let us celebrate and ascribe to Him glory and honor, for the
marriage of the Lamb [at last] has come, and His bride has
prepared herself.

—REVELATION 19:7, AMP

MARRIAGE IS BOTH SPIRITUAL AND NATURAL. IN THIS BOOK WE WILL try to explore the spiritual side of marriage to help us understand the purpose for marriage and what was in the mind of God when He created this divine institution.

There are diversities of peoples, cultures, languages, and religious persuasions in the world today. Religion, whether good or evil, is a dominant factor in every culture and continues to play an important role in shaping the culture and life-style of people in our society. The Christian world is divided into denominations that hold certain foundational truths as their rule of faith and doctrine. One truth we all agree with is that marriage is a divine institution, and it is the environment that God prescribed for children to be nurtured in and develop into adulthood.

Not all people in the non-Christian world subscribe to the same family structure and values, and many support other theories and belief systems regarding marriage, the structure of the home, and the family. However, this book was written to the Bible-believing Christians in our society. Once again, God is stirring up our minds by bringing to our remembrance why He ordained marriage and the family in the first place.

Every segment of society has had their say about marriage, divorce, and the role of women. But as we look into God's Word, we find that God, who is the Alpha and Omega, the beginning and the end of all things, had the first word about the institution of marriage, and He will also have the last word.

The church is the betrothed bride of Christ, and at the appointed time, what began in the Garden of Eden will culminate with Jesus Christ, God's Son, marrying His bride in His Father's house. The wedding arrangements have all been made, invitations have been sent out, the bride is preparing herself for the glorious event, the marriage feast is being prepared, the bridal party is almost ready, anticipation is high, and the bridegroom's arrival is imminent.

While we await the Bridegroom, God is doing a work of grace among women. The woman is the natural adaptation of the bride of Christ, who is spirit. As the natural wife is to the natural husband, so is the church to Jesus Christ. As Eve was to the first Adam, so is the church to the last Adam. God is doing a simultaneous work of healing, deliverance, and restoration with the natural woman and with His church, the spiritual woman.

The Bible indicates that Jesus will present His church to the Father as a glorious bride without spot or wrinkle. Spots and wrinkles denote character faults and sins. For all have sinned and come short of the glory of God (Rom. 3:23). Sin has hindered the church from being that beautiful, glorious bride that she is destined to be. But Jesus is cleansing His bride with the washing of water through the Word (Eph. 5:26).

God is also going back to Eden, the place of first things, to restore the natural woman to the state of wholeness and completeness in Him. She represents the female characteristics and attributes of the Godhead. The curse levied at the woman in the Garden of Eden has to be broken. All the antagonism by Satan and mankind against the woman has to be dealt with. There is a movement of the Spirit of God among women as God reproduces Himself in them. He is anointing the women in the body of Christ and bringing them to the state of *shalom* (peace). Even now there is a cry among women for deliverance from oppression, gender prejudice, abuse, control, and bondage.

God has not forgotten about the curse He placed on the woman after the Fall. To the serpent He said, "'I will put enmity between you and the woman, and between your offspring and hers; he will crush your head, and you will strike his heel.' To the woman he said, 'I will greatly increase your pains in childbearing; with pain you will give birth to children. Your desire will be for your husband, and he will rule over you'" (Gen. 3:15–16, NIV).

When God heard the cries, groanings, afflictions, and travail of the children of Israel in Egyptian bondage, He sent a deliverer. Every time a woman travails to bring forth a child, her cry goes up to God. There is a similar cry that comes out of the soul of the church, the bride of Christ; for as soon as Zion (the church) travails, she brings forth her children. God has heard the cry of women for deliverance from oppression in the city, oppression in the home, oppression in the marketplace, oppression in the house of God, and oppression in every walk of life where Satan has reared his head against the woman and her seed.

The Father is responding to the cries of the natural and spiritual woman. He is revisiting Eden, taking us back to the place where He originally designed and created the holy estate of matrimony between the male and the female. When God instituted marriage, He established it upon the law of agreement and the law of love. These two laws are the bond and fellowship of this union.

From the fall of man until the present age, there have been many attacks from the powers of darkness to redefine marriage, such as polygamy, divorce, and cohabitation without covenant, all of which strike at the original plan and intent of God.

In many ancient cultures and in biblical times, polygamy was an accepted tradition and custom of family life. It was and still is a stronghold in many ancient cultures and segments of society. Wealthy men, kings, and tribal lords had several wives and concubines (the equivalent of a modern-day mistress). These wives and concubines bore children, and as the family enlarged, it became a tribe or a clan. As tribes grew and multiplied, they became nations having their own laws, culture, economy, land, and language.

These ancient cultures also had forms of worship that were pagan or idolatrous because they did not know the true and living God who made the heavens and the earth. Their temple rituals took the form of sexual orgies; sex with children (especially virgins); men with male prostitutes; women with women; human sacrifices; blood sacrifices with animals; cutting, branding, and placing demonic marks on the human body, humming and chanting songs of worship to their idol gods; and ritualistic dance when the body was possessed by spirit entities.

The practice of sodomy can be traced back to ancient civilization, and it is at the root of sexual perversion. Even though America was founded on Christian principles, in recent years the state of Massachusetts and many other states have begun to write laws to legalize sodomy so that same-sex individuals can legally marry. Sodomites want the same benefits and social acceptance as people in structured homogeneous relationships.

Even though sodomy continues to be a part of the culture, polygamy for the most part has been outlawed; only minor pockets of resistance remain in minute areas in various states in America, but it is still a tradition and custom in various parts of the world. However, adultery and all forms of sexual perversion are national pastimes.

The "mother of harlots" (Rev. 3:5, KJV) is at the root of all sexual perversion and idolatry. Promiscuity, sodomy, adultery, fornication, incest, pedophilia, pornography, cohabitation outside of a covenant, and divorce are all the works of the flesh.

Because of man's relentless wickedness and hardness of heart, Moses gave the men of Israel permission to divorce their wives (Deut. 24), but in the beginning, at the genesis of marriage, it was not in the mind of God; it was not God's intent (Matt. 19:8). Divorce does not conform to the original design, pattern, or plan of God for marriage and for the procreation of mankind.

In recent years when judgment came to the Roman Catholic Church, we were amazed and alarmed as the covers were pulled off of the hidden sins of the church of Rome. All her abominations, which were blatant violations of the Word of God, were open and naked for the world to see. The world sat in judgment as the hidden sins of priests and bishops were exposed. The Protestant churches have had their share of violations and compromise also. They too are guilty of hiding their sins of harlotry under the covers and sweeping their infidelity under the carpet.

Marriage is a noble and divine institution that was ordained by God. He intended marriage to be a benefit and blessing to mankind, but because of man's fallen, unrighteous, sinful state, man is prone to disobedience and lawlessness. Therefore, Moses had to include a rider in the law, which allowed a husband to divorce his wife. But in this season, once again, God is going back to Eden, the place of first things, to remind His church and His people that there is a biblical pattern and a spiritual principle involved in marriage.

> Let marriage be held in honor (esteemed worthy, precious, of great price, and especially dear) in all things. And thus let the marriage bed be undefiled (kept undishonored); for God will judge and punish the unchaste [all guilty of sexual vice] and adulterous.
>
> —HEBREWS 13:4

For the time [has arrived] for judgment to begin with the household of
God; and if it begins with us, what will [be] the end of those who do
not respect or believe or obey the good news (the Gospel) of God?
—1 PETER 4:17

Every lawless segment of the kingdom of man has had their say about
marriage and has lived contrary to God's plan. Now God is about to have His
say about His divine institution, and He is speaking through His church.

I give you a new commandment: that you should love one another.
Just as I have loved you, so you too should love one another.
By this shall all [men] know that you are My disciples, if you love
one another [if you keep on showing love among yourselves].
—JOHN 13:34–35

He gave His church a new commandment to love one another. This law
rings true not only as a principle for the sons of God to live by, but also as a
pivotal truth in the covenant of marriage. This law also states that by love we
must serve one another (Gal. 5:13). Love is the bond of maturity.

My intention in writing this book is for the church—which the Bible calls
a chosen generation, a royal priesthood, a holy nation, and a peculiar people—
to go back to Eden to take a look at God's original plan, design, and purpose
for relationship in the covenant of marriage. This needs to be done so that we
may understand how Satan, in his blatant attempt to sabotage God's design
for the family and his timeless efforts to corrupt the seed of the man and the
woman, has debased and turned this form of true worship into an idolatrous
worship of corruptible flesh.

In his letter to the church at Rome, the apostle Paul spoke emphatically
about the righteousness of God and God's indignation against unrighteousness in the corrupt, immoral society that Rome was known to be.

For God's [holy] wrath and indignation are revealed from heaven
against all ungodliness and unrighteousness of men, who in their
wickedness repress and hinder the truth and make it inoperative.
For that which is known about God is evident to them and made
plain in their inner consciousness, because God [Himself] has shown
it to them.

For ever since the creation of the world His invisible nature and attributes, that is, His eternal power and divinity, have been made intelligible and clearly discernible in and through the things that have been made (His handiworks). So [men] are without excuse [altogether without any defense or justification], because when they knew and recognized Him as God, they did not honor and glorify Him as God or give Him thanks. But instead they became futile and godless in their thinking [with vain imaginings, foolish reasoning, and stupid speculations] and their senseless minds were darkened.

Claiming to be wise, they became fools [professing to be smart, they made simpletons of themselves].

And by them the glory and majesty and excellence of the immortal God were exchanged for and represented by images, resembling mortal man and birds and beasts and reptiles.

Therefore God gave them up in the lusts of their [own] hearts to sexual impurity, to the dishonoring of their bodies among themselves [abandoning them to the degrading power of sin], because they exchanged the truth of God for a lie and worshiped and served the creature rather than the Creator, Who is blessed forever! Amen (so be it).

For this reason God gave them over and abandoned them to vile affections and degrading passions. For their women exchanged their natural function for an unnatural and abnormal one, and the men also turned from natural relations with women and were set ablaze (burning out, consumed) with lust for one another, men committing shameful acts with men and suffering in their own bodies and personalities the inevitable consequences and penalty of their wrong-doing and going astray, which was [their] fitting retribution.

And so, since they did not see fit to acknowledge God or approve of Him or consider Him worth knowing, God gave them over to a base and condemned mind to do things not proper or decent but loathsome, until they were filled (permeated and saturated) with every kind of unrighteousness, iniquity, grasping and covetous greed, and malice. [They were] full of envy and jealousy, murder, strife, deceit and treachery, ill will and cruel ways. [They were] secret backbiters and gossipers, slanderers, hateful to and hating God, full of insolence, arrogance, [and] boasting; inventors of new forms of evil, disobedient and undutiful to parents.

[They were] without understanding, conscienceless and faithless, heartless and loveless [and] merciless.

Though they are fully aware of God's righteous decree that those who do such things deserve to die, they not only do them themselves but approve and applaud others who practice them.

—ROMANS 1:18–32

This word, though spoken about a corrupt, immoral Roman society, is also relevant for today's hedonistic culture. Love, respect, honesty, morality, and fidelity in the marriage covenant are the pillars that uphold the union. These virtues are becoming more and more socially unacceptable. Many people who have been married for quite a long time are finding themselves in the minority. In Western society and in some cultures around the world, if one remains married for over ten years, it is considered quite an achievement.

When my youngest daughter was in elementary school she made an observation and remarked to me one day, "Mom, how is it that you and Daddy are still married?" I said, "Why do you ask that question?" She said, "Only two other children in my class live with their father and mother."

Chapter 1

THE ORIGINAL PLAN

For every house is builded by some man; but he that built all things is God.

—Hebrews 3:4, kjv

God is a master builder, and everything He designs and creates is according to a pattern and based upon a principle. The design, blueprints, and pattern for all that God created and instituted in the earth are in the heavenlies. Heaven is His throne, and the earth is His footstool. The earth was created as a prototype of the kingdom of heaven, and it is the environment in which God placed the male and the female to take dominion by occupying, possessing, building, planting, procreating, and using its vast resources.

The earth sphere is the kingdom of man. As Creator, God enacted spiritual and natural laws to govern the kingdom of man and all of creation. His intent was that the kingdom of man on Earth would be aligned with the principles, patterns, and laws of the kingdom of heaven. In teaching His disciples how to pray, Jesus said, "When ye pray, say...Thy kingdom come. Thy will be done, as in heaven, so in earth" (Luke 11:2, kjv).

God used Himself as the pattern when He created man. He made man in His image and likeness. The woman represents the female characteristics and attributes of God, and the man represents the male characteristics and attributes of God.

On the sixth day of Creation, the Godhead—Father, Son, and Holy Spirit—spoke to the earth in the same manner in which they spoke when they said, "Let the earth bring forth" (Gen. 1:11, kjv). Once again they addressed the earth:

> Let us [Father, Son, and Holy Spirit] make mankind in Our image, after Our likeness, and let them have complete authority over the fish of the sea, the birds of the air, the [tame] beasts, and over all of the earth, and over everything that creeps upon the earth.
>
> —Genesis 1:26

Then the Lord God formed man out of the dust of the ground and breathed into man the breath of life, and man became a living soul, unlike other creatures. But when the man sinned, God said, "For dust you are and to dust you will return" (Gen. 3:19, niv).

"Likeness" denotes that God made something with the same resemblance or similitude of Himself. "Image" denotes Godlike qualities, such as love, goodness, beauty, strength, prudence, wisdom, discretion, and courage. In other words, man was created as a visible manifestation of God in an earthly form.

The uniqueness of the Godhead is that they function in harmony as one entity. When Jesus said, "I and the Father are One" (John 10:30), He meant they are like-minded; they think exactly alike. Jesus knows the thoughts and ways of the Father because He is of the same composition, and He possesses the same attributes as the Father. They are one in class, design, character, attribute, purpose, and accord. The word *accord* is defined as mutual agreement, or harmony.

In the Book of Hebrews, the Bible declares that Jesus is the sole expression of the glory of God, the perfect imprint and very image of God's nature.

> He is the sole expression of the glory of God [the Light-being, the out-raying or radiance of the divine], and He is the perfect imprint and very image of [God's] nature, upholding and maintaining and guiding and propelling the universe by His mighty word of power. When He had by offering Himself accomplished our cleansing of sins and riddance of guilt, He sat down at the right hand of the divine Majesty on high.
>
> —Hebrews 1:3

You will find the same characteristics in the Son that you find in the Father. The Son is the exact similitude of the Father; He has the same capabilities, strengths, and aptitude as the Father. He possesses all the Father's qualities, the DNA that makes God who He is. Jesus describes it this way: "Anyone who has seen Me has seen the Father" (John 14:9). There is no difference between them except in function.

> And the Word (Christ) became flesh (human, incarnate) and tabernacled (fixed His tent of flesh, lived awhile) among us; and we [actually] saw His glory (His honor, His majesty), such glory as an only begotten son receives from his father, full of grace (favor, loving-kindness) and truth.
>
> —JOHN 1:14

Adam was God's son with the divine nature of God in an earthly body. Because of his sinless nature he was also covered by the glory of God. According to the intent of God, He created His earthly son Adam to be an expression of himself in the earth. The male and female were to be one in perfect order, harmony, love, and fellowship with the Godhead and all of creation, yet occupying separate bodies with distinct functions.

> And God blessed them and said to them, Be fruitful, multiply, and fill the earth, and subdue it [using all its vast resources in the service of God and man]; and have dominion over the fish of the sea, the birds of the air, and over every living creature that moves upon the earth.
>
> —GENESIS 1:28

Man, in his kingdom, the Garden of Eden, was in perfect harmony with God and with the ecosystem in his earthly environment. Heaven and Earth were in alignment and in agreement with God's order, and there was harmony and balance between the dimensions of spirit and earth, each corresponding, fellowshipping, and interrelating thoughts and ideas with each other. The mind of man and the mind of God were in sync.

The earth was man's inheritance. Man was given possession of and dominion over the earth. It was his kingdom to preside over, but in order for dominion to be maintained three things had to happen. One, man must keep the devil under his feet and crush his head into submission. Two, the man and his wife must remain obedient to God. And finally, their love for God and each other must be the bond of their relationship.

Before God took the rib out of the man to build the woman, God made a very key observation about man and said, "It is not good that man should be alone" (Gen. 2:18, NKJV). To everything God created He said it was good and

He blessed it, but for man, He said it was not good for man to be alone. God was not just talking about the male spending quiet time alone or going fishing by himself so that he could get away from the rat race. Alone time or quiet time is not what God had in mind.

Socially, it was not good for man to be alone. Adam was in a class all by himself, possessing the male and female attributes of God. But according to God's divine purpose for man, Adam was to be the progenitor of a breed of human beings (other sons of God). The man had to produce children similar to and in the image of their father. His children would have his spirit, as he had his Father's Spirit.

But the man was alone without another creature in his class to socialize and fellowship with. There was no one who could assist him in fulfilling his fatherly function and the purpose of God for Earth—to have sons to worship and to fellowship with him. God wanted a family of children on the earth, and this would not come to pass if the man was alone.

Adam was a father without sons, and a husband without a wife. God brought all the living creatures before Adam to see what he would call them, and Adam gave names to all of them, but for Adam, there was not found a helper or a mate suitably adapted or complementary to him. Adam needed a companion that was going in the same prophetic direction as he was. God made man to be kings and priests unto God, and even though the lion is king in the animal kingdom, the lion was not compatible to man in his position as king in the human kingdom.

Everything that Adam needed was in Eden—except a mate. He had food, water, power, authority, privilege, prestige, honor, the vast resources of Eden, the gold of Havilah, and relationship with God, yet he had no one to share his inheritance with. There in the inner recesses of his soul, the man was unfulfilled because he had the same desire that God had. He also wanted a family; he wanted children. His desire was to produce seed in his image and likeness, children who were like-minded with similar characteristics, children he could communicate his thoughts, ideas, and intentions to.

Every type of vegetation and form of life that the earth produced had seed within itself. The seed was programmed to produce fruit with seed after its kind. Man was also a product of the earth. He too had seed within himself and had the ability to produced fruit similar to himself.

> The earth brought forth vegetation: plants yielding seed according to their own kinds and trees bearing fruit in which was their seed, each according to its kind. And God saw that it was good (suitable, admirable) and He approved it.
>
> —GENESIS 1:12

God, the master builder, took a bone out of Adam and built it up and created a woman. This creature would be the receptacle and incubator of Adam's seed. Then Adam took his seed and placed it inside the woman's womb, and together they produced fruit (children). "Male and female He created them" (Gen. 1:27). This was God's design for the promulgation of the human race and for marriage. The male could not replenish the earth without the female.

A man cannot impregnate another man, nor can a woman receive seed from another woman. A man marrying another man and a woman marrying another woman is not consistent with God's original pattern for the family. It is humanistic in effort and demonic in design because it spells death to the human race. Out of that concept and plan there is no procreation, no life, no energy, and no movement toward the next generation. All it does is satisfy the most basic, depraved, lustful desire of the human flesh. Therefore, that concept is out of order with the rest of creation.

Adam (man) is the highest order of God's creation, and the male needed an Eve (female), the mother of all living human beings. No life can be produced in a same-sex union. There can be no procreation because that arrangement was not designed by God. All of God's creatures have seed. The element of life is in the seed, and all seed has this element of truth embedded and programmed into it. It must produce *life*.

> In the beginning [before all time] was the Word (Christ), and the Word was with God, and the Word was God Himself. He was present originally with God.
>
> All things were made and came into existence through Him; and without Him was not even one thing made that has come into being. In Him was Life, and the Life was the Light of men.
>
> —JOHN 1:1–4

Marriage refers to the relationship between a man and a woman who have legally become one, or husband and wife. Therefore, by definition, marriage is a union.

Man is a spirit and he has a soul, both of which are housed in a fleshly body. Marriage, therefore, is the union of two spirits, two souls, and two bodies. It is a relationship between a man and a woman who are bound together by covenant. The covenant is what legally binds them together as man and wife.

Marriage is spiritual as well as natural. According to the Bible, it is the first and oldest institution among mankind, dating back from the beginning of creation in the home of Adam and Eve, the Garden of Eden.

The plan of God was that the man and his wife would live together, independent of parents, in a lifelong union that would only be broken by death. And in this union, the man and his wife would live in love and harmony and in total agreement with heaven. They would replenish the earth by procreating, having both sons and daughters.

THE LAW OF LOVE AND THE POWER OF AGREEMENT

Within the confines of this institution lies this very powerful principle. The power of agreement is the principle or bedrock upon which marriage stands.

> Again I tell you, if two of you on earth agree (harmonize together, make a symphony together) about whatever [anything and everything] they may ask, it will come to pass and be done for them by My Father in heaven.
>
> —MATTHEW 18:19

It is the law of love and the power of agreement that makes marriage the single most interrelated and structurally strong institution that has withstood the test of time. Marriage has endured the history of civilization, the fall of man, civil unrest, world wars, cultural diversity, and religion. Marriages have brought together warring factions, tribes of people, and nations united in covenant, but it has also brought together families that are socially dysfunctional and unsuited for each other into relationship.

Historically, kings and similar rulers of nations have entered into covenants with other nations through marriage. When one member of the royal seed took their spouse from the royal seed of another nation and a child was produced from that union, the families became related by blood. That child brought about the intermingling of the bloodline. Names, first or last, were exchanged, and one royal tribe took the name of the other royal tribe, denoting that a covenant had been formed and agreed upon by the presiding elders of the tribe. In more modern times as the population exploded, the bride took the last name of her husband, a practice which is still relevant in today's society.

King Solomon of Israel, David's son and heir, married the daughter of the king of Egypt. Solomon never had wars with Egypt during his reign. He also married several other wives whom the Bible calls strange women. They were the daughters of kings from the various idolatrous nations. By joining in affinity with these nations, Solomon's kingdom was safe from attack by the surrounding nations.

> And Solomon made an alliance with Pharaoh king of Egypt and took Pharaoh's daughter and brought her into the City of David until he had finished building his own house and the house of the Lord, and the wall around Jerusalem.
>
> —1 Kings 3:1

The Bible adds another dimension to the principle of the power of agreement. Ten times more can be accomplished in the spirit of unity and in a harmonious working relationship than by one person working alone.

> O that they were wise and would see through this [present triumph] to their ultimate fate! How one could have chased a thousand, and two put ten thousand to flight?
>
> —Deuteronomy 32:29–30

In every culture, race, religious persuasion, and society, marriage and family is the primary bond of human relationship. Kingdoms, generations, dynasties, and great houses established by great men have come and gone, yet this institution has been a fixture throughout the history of the world. What began in the kingdom of man, in the Garden of Eden, will culminate in the kingdom of heaven at the marriage supper of the Lamb with the second Adam, who is the Lord Jesus Christ.

Marriage has tremendous benefits, but it also has its challenges because man does not live in a Garden of Eden environment anymore. His environment has changed, and his heart has changed, but God still wants fellowship and relationship with the sons of men, and His purpose for marriage and the family has remained the same.

What made the relationship with the first man and his wife so unique was their sinless nature, their holiness, and the essence of their being, which was love. God is love. Therefore, communication with God was not difficult. This made the Garden of Eden (delight) the perfect environment or atmosphere for a visitation from God every day because God and man were in one accord.

As redeemed sons of God, the atmosphere in our homes should be one of delight, Edenic. Eden was a kingdom environment; now the kingdom is within us. But God is seeking habitation, not just visitation in the cool of the day. God requires a harmonious relationship between the man and his wife, that they be one in corporeality, united in the bond of love, which is symbolic of Christ, the last Adam, and His bride, the church.

> So they are no longer two, but one flesh. What therefore God has joined together, let not man put asunder (separate).
> —MATTHEW 19:6

> For this reason a man shall leave his father and his mother and shall be joined to his wife, and the two shall become one flesh.
> This mystery is very great, but I speak concerning [the relation of] Christ and the church.
> —EPHESIANS 5:31–32

What the man and his wife enjoyed in Eden was a superb quality of life, a harmonious relationship, dominion, and possession of an inheritance given to them by God. This first marriage relationship was the model or the pattern and is the intent of God for every marriage relationship.

REGULATIONS FOR MARRIAGE WITHIN THE FAMILY

During the era of time after Adam's disobedience and his expulsion from the Garden of Eden and before the Law was given to Moses on Mount Sinai, man had become a law unto himself and freely married within the family bloodline to his closest relatives. Sometimes he had two or more wives from the same family, like Jacob, who married two sisters, Leah and Rachael. Abraham married his stepsister Sarah, who was his father's daughter by another mother. Isaac married his first cousin, Rebekah. When Israel became a covenant nation under God, they were warned by God not to marry their children to the idolatrous nations around them. They were to marry among the twelve tribes.

But after four hundred years in Egypt, the twelve tribes had enlarged and expanded into thousands of family units. This facilitated intertribal marriages among families that were not too closely related. On becoming a nation under God, they were given regulations relative to marriage between the tribes and among family members based on bloodline. There was a general prohibition against marriage between a man and his own flesh. The Law of God stated:

None of you shall approach anyone close of kin to have sexual relations. I am the Lord.

The nakedness of your father, which is the nakedness of your mother, you shall not uncover; she is your mother; you shall not have intercourse with her.

The nakedness of your father's wife you shall not uncover; it is your father's nakedness.

You shall not have intercourse with or uncover the nakedness of your sister, the daughter of your father or of your mother, whether born at home or born abroad.

You must not have sexual relations with your son's daughter or your daughter's daughter; their nakedness you shall not uncover, for they are your own flesh.

You must not have intercourse with your father's wife's daughter; begotten by your father, she is your sister; you shall not uncover her nakedness.

You shall not have intercourse with your father's sister; she is your father's near kinswoman.

You shall not have sexual relations with your mother's sister, for she is your mother's near kinswoman.

You shall not have intercourse with your father's brother's wife; you shall not approach his wife; she is your aunt.

You shall not uncover the nakedness of your daughter-in-law; she is your son's wife; you shall not have intercourse with her.

You shall not have intercourse with your brother's wife; she belongs to your brother.

You shall not marry a woman and her daughter, nor shall you take her son's daughter or her daughter's daughter to have intercourse; they are [her] near kinswomen; it is wickedness and an outrageous offense.

You must not marry a woman in addition to her sister, to be a rival to her, having sexual relations with the second sister when the first one is alive.

—Leviticus 18:6–18

There was one exception in favor of marriage with a brother's wife in the event that the brother died childless:

> If brothers live together and one of them died and has no son, his wife shall not be married outside the family to a stranger [an excluded man]. Her husband's brother shall go in to her and take her as his wife and perform the duty of a husband's brother to her.
>
> And the firstborn son shall succeed to the name of the dead brother, that his name may not be blotted out of Israel.
>
> And if the man does not want to take his brother's wife, then let his brother's wife go up to the gate to the elders, and say, My husband's brother refuses to continue his brother's name in Israel; he will not perform the duty of my husband's brother.
>
> Then the elders of his city shall call him and speak to him. And if he stands firm and says, I do not want to take her, then shall his brother's wife come to him in the presence of the elders and pull his shoe off his foot and spit in his face and shall answer, So shall it be done to that man who does not build up his brother's house.
>
> And his family shall be called in Israel, The House of Him Whose Shoe Was Loosed.
>
> —DEUTERONOMY 25:5–10

Jesus came as the last Adam. The Bible says the first shall be last and the last shall be first (Mark 10:31). The first Adam was the progenitor of the human race, but he died because of his transgression. Jesus, who was born of God like the first Adam, not after the will of man or the will of the flesh, but of God, came into the earth as Adam's brother to fulfill or to complete the assignment of the first Adam in raising sons. As Christ, Jesus restored spiritual life to man who was dead in trespasses and sins. As Adam, Jesus became the progenitor of a generation of sons of God in the earth, born of the incorruptible seed of the Word of God. Jesus Christ took the place of the first Adam, and the last Adam became first.

> The first man Adam became a living being (an individual personality); the last Adam (Christ) became a life-giving Spirit [restoring the dead to life].
>
> —1 CORINTHIANS 15:45

The name *Adam* (man) is generic, for it is not confined to the father of the human race but was applicable to the woman as well as to the man, and it is inclusive of the entire human race. The first Adam's generation was born after the flesh, spiritually dead, spiritually disconnected from the life source, which is God, because of the first Adam's disobedience and sin. But in Christ, the last Adam, all were made alive. Christ produced a generation of sons who were born of the Spirit and the incorruptible seed of the Word of God.

> You have been regenerated (born again), not from a mortal origin (seed, sperm), but from one that is immortal by the ever living and lasting Word of God.
>
> —1 PETER 1:23

THE MYSTERY OF CHRIST AND THE CHURCH

The relationship of the natural woman to her husband is relative to the spiritual woman (the church) and her husband, Jesus Christ. The natural precedes the spiritual. First, there was the natural man and his wife, Adam and Eve, who are symbolic of Jesus Christ and His bride, the church.

> But it is not the spiritual life which cam first, but the physical and then the spiritual.
>
> —1 CORINTHIANS 15:46

God never built the human body to die. Death only became an option when man sinned by disobeying the law God instituted in the Garden of Eden, a law that specifically stated, "But of the tree of the knowledge of good and evil…you shall not eat, for in the day that you eat of it you shall surely die" (Gen. 2:17). Death is the result or the wages of sin. There is a natural death that occurs when the spirit of the man goes back to God and the natural body goes back to the earth. There is also a spiritual death, a state that someone is born into when the body is physically alive but the spirit is dead due to sin and alienated from the life of God.

Through his self-indulgence, the first Adam blatantly disobeyed the commandment of God, and by doing so, the generations that were in his loins, which had his DNA, would all be subjected to spiritual and physical death like their forefather Adam. Every human being in all the generations of man that would be born into the earth would be born in the state of spiritual death and alienated from the life of God. To correct the problem God sent the last Adam who was a living Spirit to undo the dead works of the first Adam.

> For as in Adam all die, even so in Christ shall all be made alive.
> —1 Corinthians 15:22, kjv

The church is the spiritual adaptation of the natural woman. There is a natural woman, and there is a spiritual woman. The spiritual woman is the body of Christ, the church. As the natural man and his wife are one flesh, Christ and the church are one spirit. As the natural man tends and cares for his wife, his natural body, so the Lord Jesus tends and cares for His wife, His spiritual body.

> Even so husbands should love their wives as [being in a sense] their own bodies. He who loves his own wife loves himself.
> For no man ever hated his own flesh, but nourishes and carefully protects and cherishes it, as Christ does the church.
> —Ephesians 5:28–29

Revelation 12 gives us an insight of the spiritual woman pregnant with child. The vision John saw of a pregnant woman crying out with birth pains in the anguish of delivery is symbolic. It is reflective of the natural woman during her time of delivery as she cries out in her anguish and pain. As the natural woman goes through the birthing process, she is bringing forth the seed of the natural man. As the spiritual woman goes through her birthing process, she is bringing forth the seed of her spiritual husband.

> And great sign (wonder)—[warning of future events of ominous significance] appeared in heaven: a woman clothed with the sun, with the moon under her feet, and with a crownlike garland (tiara) of twelve stars on her head.
> She was pregnant and she cried out in her birth pangs, in the anguish of her delivery.
> —Revelation 12:1–2

The natural woman's womb is the legal doorway of entry into the earth realm. To come into the earth by any other means is an illegal entry. Even God, the anointed Christ, had to come through the doorway of a woman's womb to legally taste death for every man.

Then the angel said to her, The Holy Spirit will come upon you, and the power of the Most High will overshadow you [like a shining cloud]; and so the holy (pure, sinless) Thing (Offspring) which shall be born of you will be called the Son of God.

—Luke 1:35

While in Eden, Adam made a declaration that was a directive for all of his sons to adhere to in their generations to come. Adam said:

Therefore a man shall leave his father and his mother and shall become united and cleave to his wife, and they shall become one flesh.

—Genesis 2:24

When the man Jesus, the last Adam, came into the earth, He too had to conform to the directives of the first Adam concerning the relationship of the man to his wife. The first Adam did not have a mother or an earthly father. What he had was a spiritual Father and a league with the earth. All of his sons would have features and definitions that were of the earth.

Before the earth was cursed, she gave birth to all the animals, trees, and flying fowl. In union with God the Father, she gave birth to the first man, giving him his earthly features and distinctive physical characteristics. When Cain killed Abel, he became part of the curse that God levied against the earth because of Adam's disobedience. The earth had opened its mouth to receive the blood of Abel. The life is in the blood, and the voice of the blood of Abel was crying out to God for justice.

And now you are cursed by reason of the earth, which has opened its mouth to receive your brother's [shed] blood from your hand.

When you till the ground, it shall no longer yield to you its strength; you shall be a fugitive and a vagabond on the earth [in perpetual exile, a degraded outcast].

—Genesis 4:11–12

As the progenitor and father of the human race, Adam had the authority to set the policy and speak on behalf of his sons, who were still in his loins. Before his transgression, Adam knew the mind, heart, and plan of God for his sons. Eden was a heavenly place, a kingdom environment that was uncontaminated by evil. Adam was able to have the same thought patterns that God had in this uncorrupted, pristine environment. Adam did not have to pray to get the mind of God. He was on the frequency of heaven all the time, and God's thoughts were his thoughts. He understood divine principles and patterns, and in his position of father, king, and husband, Adam had the authority to declare in the earth and prophesy to the generations that were to come, that a man shall leave his father and his mother and shall become united to his wife, and they shall become one flesh. Jesus Christ had to honor the word of the first Adam, therefore, He said to His bride:

> For I am going away to prepare a place for you. And when (if) I go and make ready a place for you, I will come back again and will take you to Myself, that where I am you may be also.
>
> —JOHN 14:2–3

The first five books of the Bible, the Torah, were the marriage contract God had with Israel. God, according to His covenant with Abraham, brought his descendants out of Egypt, assembled them together on Mount Sinai, and gave them a constitution and laws that made them a nation under God. Then God entered into a covenant relationship with them, marrying Himself to that nation. After accepting the covenant, the people sanctified and prepared themselves for the third day when the Lord would come down on the mountain to ratify the covenant. God came down in a thick cloud, a canopy, accompanied by fire. The cloud and the pillar of fire remained a fixture over Israel as a sign of the marriage covenant God had with her. As Israel was the bride of God, so the church is the bride of Christ. (See Exodus 19.)

> You [Judah] shall no more be termed Forsaken, nor shall your land be called Desolate any more. But you shall be called Hephzibah [My delight is in her], and your land be called Beulah [married]; for the Lord delights in you, and your land shall be married [owned and protected by the Lord].
>
> For as a young man marries a virgin [O Jerusalem], so shall your sons marry you; and as the bridegroom rejoices over the bride, so shall your God rejoice over you.
>
> —ISAIAH 62:4–5

For thy Maker is thine husband; the LORD of hosts is his name; and thy Redeemer the Holy One of Israel; the God of the whole earth shall he be called.

—ISAIAH 54:5, KJV

THE ANCIENT HEBREW WEDDING

As the Son of God and His heir apparent, Jesus Christ laid the foundation of His church by choosing twelve disciples, who he called apostles. There are twelve apostles of the new covenant, as there were twelve tribes of Israel under the old covenant. The prophets of the old covenant and the apostles of the new covenant are the foundation of the church, and the church is referred to as the bride of Christ.

The marriage of Isaac and Rebekah is an Old Testament–type of Hebrew wedding, which is symbolic of the espousal of Christ and His church. In historical times, the choice of the bride was not always the responsibility of the bridegroom himself, but his family members also assisted him. Occasionally, the whole business of selecting the wife was left in the hands of a family friend. As a father, Abraham took the responsibility of seeking a wife for his son Isaac. A wife would ensure the promulgation of the promise seed, the generational blessing of his ancestral bloodline and the fulfillment of the promises of God.

> Now Abraham was old, well advanced in years, and the Lord had blessed Abraham in all things. And Abraham said to the eldest servant of his house [Eliezer of Damascus], who ruled over all that he had, I beg of you, put your hand under my thigh; and you shall swear by the Lord, the God of heaven and earth, that you will not take a wife for my son from the daughters of the Canaanites, among whom I have settled, but you shall go to my country and to my relatives and take a wife for my son Isaac.
>
> —GENESIS 24:1–4

The consent of the maiden was asked, but the consent of the father and older brother was of paramount importance because it is the father or older brother that spoke the word of blessing into the life of their daughter or sister.

> And they said, We will call the girl and ask her [what is] her desire. So they called Rebekah and said to her, Will you go with this man?

And she said, I will go. So they sent away Rebekah their sister and her nurse [Deborah] and Abraham's servant and his men.

And they blessed Rebekah and said to her, You are our sister; may you become the mother of thousands of ten thousands, and let your posterity possess the gate of their enemies.

—GENESIS 24:57–60

The first stage in the ancient Hebrew wedding was the selection of the bride and the espousal. This was the formal contractual agreement that settled the price the bridegroom had to pay for the bride. It was confirmed by oaths and accompanied by presents to the bride. This formal proceeding was undertaken by a friend or legal representative on behalf of the bridegroom and by the parents on behalf of the bride. This act of betrothal was celebrated by a feast.

Christ selected His bride when He was on Earth. He celebrated the act of betrothal at the Last Supper or Passover feast with His apostles (the church) before He went to the cross. During the feast, Jesus drank from the silver cup. Silver symbolized the price of redemption. With that covenant meal, He sealed the marriage contract. On the cross, Jesus paid the price of redemption for His bride with His own life and blood.

And He said to them, I have earnestly and intensely desired to eat this Passover with you before I suffer; for I say to you, I shall eat it no more until it is fulfilled in the kingdom of God.

And He took a cup, and when He had given thanks, He said, Take this and divide and distribute it among yourselves; for I say to you that from now on I shall not drink of the fruit of the vine at all until the kingdom of God comes.

—LUKE 22:15–18

After the distribution of gifts, the bridegroom departs and goes to his father's house. He will not return again until the father says it is time, for only the father knows the day and the hour when his son shall return for his bride. While the bridegroom tarries, the bride goes through the process of purification, sanctification, and consecration, making herself ready for his return.

Husbands, love your wives, as Christ loved the church and gave Himself up for her, so that He might sanctify her, having cleansed her by the washing of water with the Word, that He might present

the church to Himself in glorious splendor, without spot or wrinkle or
any such things [that she might be holy and faultless].

—EPHESIANS 5:25–27

The second stage of the Hebrew marriage is called the invitation, or the
taking and receiving of the bride. The bride is invited to the father's house. For
the church, this will begin with the Rapture and conclude with Christ at the
marriage supper in heaven.

And the servant brought out jewels of silver, jewels of gold, and
garments and gave them to Rebekah; he also gave precious things to
her brother and her mother.
Then they ate and drank, he and the men who were with him, and
stayed there all night. And in the morning they arose, and he said.
Send me away to my master.
And Rebekah and her maids arose and followed the man upon
their camels. Thus the servant took Rebekah and went on his way.

—GENESIS 24:53–54, 61

Between the betrothal and the marriage, an interval elapsed, varying from
a few days in the patriarchal age to a full year for virgins and a month for
widows in later times. During this period, the bride-elect lived with her friends
or relatives, and all communication between herself and her future husband
was carried on through a relative or friend chosen for the purpose, known as
the "friend of the bridegroom."

The bride belongs to the bridegroom. The friend who attends the
bridegroom waits and listens for him, and is full of joy when he hears
the bridegroom's voice. That joy is mine, and it is now complete.

—JOHN 3:29, NIV

The bride was now virtually regarded as the wife of her future husband;
hence, unfaithfulness on her part was punishable with death. The husband
also had the option of "putting her away."

Now the birth of Jesus Christ took place under these circumstances:
When His mother Mary had been promised in marriage to Joseph,
before they came together, she was found to be pregnant [through the
power] of the Holy Spirit.

And her [promised] husband Joseph, being a just and upright man and not willing to expose her publicly and to shame and disgrace her, decided to repudiate and dismiss (divorce) her quietly and secretly.

—Matthew 1:18–19

When a man takes a wife and marries her, if then she finds no favor in his eyes because he has found some indecency in her, and he writes her a bill of divorce, puts it in her hand, and sends her out of his house.

—Deuteronomy 24:1

As the Bridegroom, Jesus had to leave His betrothed for a little while. He departed with the promise that He was going to prepare a place for the bride but will return to receive her unto Himself.

The essence of the marriage ceremony consisted in the removal of the bride from her father's house to that of the bridegroom or his father's house. The bridegroom prepared himself for the occasion by putting on a festive dress and by placing on his head a handsome nuptial turban.

At the house a feast was prepared, to which all the friends and neighbors were invited and the festivities were carried out for seven or even fourteen days. The guests were provided with fitting robes by the host, and the feast was enlivened with riddles and other amusements.

Let us rejoice and shout for joy [exulting and triumphant]! Let us celebrate and ascribe to Him glory and honor, for the marriage of the Lamb [at last] has come, and His bride has prepared herself.

She has been permitted to dress in fine (radiant) linen, dazzling and white—for the fine linen is (signifies, represents) the righteousness (the upright, just, and godly living, deeds, and conduct, and right standing with God) of the saints (God's holy people).

Then [the angel] said to me, Write this down: Blessed (happy, to be envied) are those who are summoned (invited, called) to the marriage supper of the Lamb. And he said to me [further], These are the true words (the genuine and exact declarations) of God.

—Revelation 19:7–9

The bride was veiled. Her robes were white, and sometimes embroidered with gold thread, and covered with perfumes. She was also decked out with jewels. When the fixed hour arrived, which was generally late in the evening, the bridegroom left his house attended by his groomsmen. They were preceded by a band of musicians or singers and accompanied by persons bearing lamps. He would then take the bride along with his friends to his own house for the celebration.

> Then shall the kingdom of heaven be likened unto ten virgins, which took their lamps, and went forth to meet the bridegroom....
> And at midnight there was a cry made, Behold, the bridegroom cometh; go ye out to meet him.
> —MATTHEW 25:1, 6, KJV

Most bridegrooms came at night, but he sent his friend to announce that he was on his way. The bridegroom and his friends went and brought the bride from her father's house to his own house, where the feast was held. The last act in the ceremony was the conducting of the bride to the bridal chamber, where a canopy, or *huppah*, was prepared. The bride was still completely veiled so that the deception practiced on Jacob was not difficult.

> And Rebekah looked up, and when she saw Isaac, she dismounted from the camel.
> For she [had] said to the servant, Who is that man walking across the field to meet us? And the servant [had] said, He is my master. So she took a veil and concealed herself with it.
> And the servant told Isaac everything that he had done.
> And Isaac brought her into his mother Sarah's tent, and he took Rebekah and she became his wife, and he loved her; thus Isaac was comforted after his mother's death.
> —GENESIS 24:64–67

The ancient Hebrew wedding is a depiction of the marriage between Christ and the church. Among the more modern Jews, it is the custom, in some parts, for the bridegroom to place a ring on the bride's finger. The ring was regarded among the Hebrews as a token of fidelity and of adoption into a family. But in the kingdom of God it is symbolic of covenant. The apostle Paul said, "This mystery is very great, but I speak concerning [the relation of] Christ and the church" (Eph. 5:32).

> However, let each man of you [without exception] love his wife as [being in a sense] his very own self; and let the wife see that she respects

and reverences her husband [that she notices him, regards him, honors him, prefers him, venerates, and esteems him; and that she defers to him, praises him, and loves and admires him exceedingly].

—Ephesians 5:33

When Jesus told His church, "I will drink no more of the fruit of the vine, until that day that I drink it new in the kingdom of God" (Mark 14:25, kjv), He was making reference to His own marriage feast, when as the Bridegroom, He will drink of the fruit of the vine in celebration of the glorious event, His marriage to the church.

The fruit of the vine was a common food of the Israelites in both Old and New Testament times. It was one of the articles they offered to God in sacrifice. They considered a good supply of wine, along with other articles of daily food, to be God's blessings. Wine was associated with joy and merriment; therefore, it was the beverage of choice at wedding feasts. Wine was also the beverage of choice for kings. Wine is symbolic of the anointing of the Holy Spirit.

At the celebration feast of the wedding at Cana, Jesus performed His first miracle, which was the turning of water into wine. (See John 2:1–11.) This too is symbolic. In her unpurified state, the church is being washed with the water of the Word. But in her glorious state, instead of drinking and washing with water, she will be celebrating with her husband and drinking the new wine of the spirit in the kingdom of God. It was a prophetic revelation when the governor of the feast remarked that they had saved the best wine for last. The best wine will be served in the kingdom of Heaven at the marriage supper of the Lamb.

Chapter 2

THE ROLE OF FATHERS

Listen, my sons, to a father's instruction; pay attention and gain understanding. Get wisdom, get understanding; do not forget my words or swerve from them.

—PROVERBS 4:1, 5

AFTER I GRADUATED FROM HIGH SCHOOL, MY IMMEDIATE PLANS WERE to migrate, go to college, and live independently of my parents. But in my haste to get on with my life, I left home without securing the prayers and blessings of my father. My new home was Washington DC, the governmental headquarters of the United States. I rented an apartment and began to build my new life, going to school and working part time, but each time I entered my apartment, I would inadvertently look up. The strangest thing was happening: it seemed as though when I looked up, I was seeing right through the ceiling and staring at the sky. There was no roof over my head, even though there was an entire fourth floor of apartments above my third-floor apartment.

I eventually prayed to God for the answer to this perplexing situation. His response to me was, "You left your covering." I came from a Christian home, yet I made the mistake of leaving home and migrating to a strange land without my father speaking his blessings over my life. As I acknowledged my mistake, I had to go back to my father's house to secure his blessing, approval, and his prayers to cover me before I could leave home the second time.

The role of fathers, or father figures, in the homes, communities, and churches is one of our most priceless assets. However, in many homes and communities, children live in households where there are no fathers or father figures. Fathers must take a more active role in the overall development of their children, primarily their education. The more fathers are involved, the fewer behavioral problems we will have in our schools and communities. Some of the many roles of a father are provider, protector, shield, and covering for his family.

A covering is the first line of defense for the body from outside elements or attack (a coat, for example). It provides security and protection. It denotes something like a veil or a mantle thrown around a body like a vesture or clothing. It is similar to a kind of shelter or roofing.

> Then the cloud [the Shekinah, God's visible presence] covered the Tent of Meeting, and the glory of the Lord filled the tabernacle!...For throughout all their journeys the cloud of the Lord was upon the tabernacle by day, and fire was in it by night, in the sight of all the house of Israel.
>
> —EXODUS 40:34, 38

God is a Father. God dwells in a realm that is invisible to the natural eye, but He manifests His presence among His children in various ways. When the children of Israel journeyed through the wilderness, God's presence among them was manifested by a cloud cover during the day. The cloud protected them during the day from the severe climatic conditions of the wilderness, which were exorbitant heat, dust, sand, wind, and dryness. At night, the wilderness would experience an extreme drop in temperature, and the covering of the Lord would appear as fire in the cloud, which provided light, heat, and protection from wild beasts.

The cloud and the pillar of fire were natural and spiritual coverings because the children of Israel were constantly under the watchful eye of the kingdom of darkness, whose strategy was to tempt the people of God to practice sin so that they would abort their divine destiny and die prematurely in the wilderness. Sin caused a breach in the covenant they had with God, which always resulted in punishment and death.

God's presence was in the cloud, and when the cloud moved, it was a signal to the children of Israel that it was time to move on. When the cloud stood still, the children of Israel stopped their journeying and set up their camp. Throughout their wilderness journey, they received their directions from the Lord by following the cloud.

In all their journeys, whenever the cloud was taken up from over the tabernacle, the Israelites went onward; but if the cloud was not taken up, they did not journey on till the day that it was taken up.

For throughout all their journeys the cloud of the Lord was upon the tabernacle by day, and fire was in it by night, in the sight of all the house of Israel.

—EXODUS 40:36–38

Joseph, the husband of Mary, who was the mother of Jesus, is a perfect example of the role of a husband and father as covering and protector because (a) His ministry was that of a father, (b) he was the husband of a woman who was pregnant with a child that was not his own, (c) he took full responsibility for the care of the mother and the child, and (d) the assignment came from God.

Now the birth of Jesus Christ took place under these circumstances: When His mother Mary had been promised in marriage to Joseph, before they came together, she was found to be pregnant [through the power] of the Holy Spirit.

And her [promised] husband Joseph, being a just and upright man and not willing to expose her publicly and to shame and disgrace her, decided to repudiate and dismiss (divorce) her quietly and secretly.

But as he was thinking this over, behold, an angel of the Lord appeared to him in a dream, saying, Joseph, descendant of David, do not be afraid to take Mary [as] your wife, for that which is conceived in her is of (from, out of) the Holy Spirit.

She will bear a Son, and you shall call His name Jesus [the Greek form of the Hebrew Joshua, which means Savior], for He will save His people from their sins [that is, prevent them from failing and missing the true end and scope of life, which is God].

But he had no union with her as her husband until she had borne her firstborn Son; and he called His name Jesus.

—MATTHEW 1:18–21, 25

When Joseph accepted his assignment, he became the covering and protector not only for Mary but also for the son she was carrying. Joseph was chosen of God to be Mary's husband and the earthly father of the Son of God. Throughout the story of Jesus's birth and in His early years in Judah and Egypt, Joseph's assignment concerning the child and His mother was given to him by an angel. Joseph was given the responsibility of fathering a child who would change the destiny of mankind.

Fathering is a divine calling and a ministry. There are many men that are not just natural fathers, but they are also spiritual fathers. Spiritual fathers nurture and develop spiritual sons. It is an honor when God gives a man an assignment to raise a child he has not biologically fathered. An assignment of that magnitude will come because of (a) the call of God on the man's life and the call of God on the child's life, (b) the anointing and ministry of the man and the anointing and destiny of the child, and (c) when the father (either natural or spiritual) is deceased or may have abandoned his position and responsibilities.

David, son of Jesse, called King Saul father and served him during the tenure of his ministry as king of Israel. David highly regarded King Saul and honored him as the anointed of the Lord. After David defeated and killed Goliath in battle, David was given the opportunity to serve under the king as a captain in the army of Israel. At first, Saul loved David and took him into his inner circle, and David became his personal psalmist. This was David's opportunity to learn about the responsibilities and official duties of a king, and it became an opportunity for Saul to be a mentor and a father to David. But Saul could not carry out his fatherly assignment because Saul was envious of David's anointing. Saul spent his latter years in office conspiring to kill David. Saul abandoned his position and assignment as a father because of his rage and jealousy toward David.

This caused David and his family to live in exile until Saul's death. However, David continued to pursue the heart of God, and according to the prophecy of Samuel concerning David, God set him on the throne of Israel after Saul's death in fulfillment of His Word.

Raising seed (children) is natural and spiritual. There are natural fathers, and there are spiritual fathers. The natural precedes the spiritual. A natural truth in the physical dimension runs parallel to a spiritual truth in the spiritual dimension. As many natural fathers have abandoned their seed and aborted their assignment to raise their children, many spiritual fathers have also aborted their assignment or have spilled their seed by abandoning their responsibility through selfishness, jealousy, ignorance, or carelessness.

However, even after Saul's death there was a long war between the house of Saul and the house of David, but Saul's house got weaker and weaker, and

David's house got stronger and stronger. (See 2 Samuel 3:1.) Saul was a father, a man of honor, who had no understanding of who he was and the nature of his assignment. "A man who is held in honor and understands not is like the beasts that perish" (Ps. 49:20).

God is a Father, and He has great love for all children. When a man of God marries a woman who has children from a previous relationship and their natural father has abandoned his responsibilities or is deceased, God will give the responsibility of fathering to the man of God with a father's heart. The destiny of those children will now be in his hands, and by assuming the responsibility, he becomes accountable to God in his capacity as the head of that household as he nurtures those children in the fear of God. If he is a just man like Joseph, his fatherly instincts and anointing will assume the responsibility because fathering has more to do with the heart of a man than his biological function as a man. A boss does not love, but a father loves unconditionally regardless of whether the children are grateful.

It was easy for Joseph to assume the role of father to Mary's son, Jesus, because Joseph had the heart of a father. The Bible describes him as a just man. *Just* denotes upright, righteous, fair, and reasonable. Joseph understood the delicate condition of Mary, a young woman pregnant with her first child and still a virgin! Being a just man, Joseph did not consummate his marriage until his wife gave birth to her firstborn son (Matt. 1:25). Her delicate condition and needs were far more important than his. Joseph's focus was on obeying God and caring for his pregnant wife and child because he understood his assignment.

Joseph was not a preacher. He was a father; this was his ministry. His wife was the chosen vessel that carried the anointed One, the Christ, redeemer of mankind. Joseph was no less important because the anointing was in and upon his wife. The church has not taught men that fathering is a ministry. Many men are called to preach, and that remains their primary focus, even if they have a family, but like Joseph, some are called to the vital ministry of fatherhood, a term that denotes maturity and godly wisdom.

> After all, though you should have ten thousand teachers (guides to direct you) in Christ, yet you do not have many fathers. For I became your father in Christ Jesus through the glad tidings (the Gospel).
> —1 Corinthians 4:15

Joseph's assignment came with some inconveniences, but Joseph was obedient to God. He did whatever God told him to do. God had a plan of redemption and restoration for the benefit of mankind, and Joseph was a part of that plan. His fatherly heart did not want any evil to overtake the child or his mother.

> Now after they had gone, behold, an angel of the Lord appeared to Joseph in a dream and said, Get up! [Tenderly] take unto you the young Child and His mother and flee to Egypt; and remain there till I tell you [otherwise], for Herod intends to search for the Child in order to destroy Him. And having risen, he took the Child and His mother by night and withdrew to Egypt And remained there until Herod's death. This was to fulfill what the Lord had spoken by the prophet, Out of Egypt have I called My Son.
>
> —Matthew 2:13–15, amp

> But when Herod died, behold, an angel of the Lord appeared in a dream to Joseph in Egypt and said, Rise, [tenderly] take unto you the Child and His mother and go to the land of Israel, for those who sought the Child's life are dead.
>
> Then he awoke and arose and [tenderly] took the Child and His mother and came into the land of Israel.
>
> —Matthew 2:19–21

After Jesus was twelve years old, nothing was ever mentioned in the Scriptures again about Joseph, but we know that he completed his assignment, which was to care for the Christ child. God, in turn, blessed him and Mary with children of their own.

In the natural, at the age of maturity, a man has to leave his father and mother, marry, and raise his own family. It is a divine plan for the natural progression of life. This is a pivotal truth not only in the natural but also in the spirit. Many spiritual parents do not understand that this principle applies to spiritual children also. Spiritual children must grow up and mature in the things of God. They must put on Christ, accept their call into the ministry, and begin to produce spiritual seed and raise spiritual children. Even after mature children have left the home, the ministry of fathering and mentoring continues into the next generation.

This truth of fathering children that were not derived from the loins of a man also has a spiritual adaptation. Many spiritual fathers in the body of Christ have assumed responsibility of fathering seed that did not come from their spiritual loins, but these spiritual children were given to them by God so that as a father, the man of God could assist in developing the leader in these children of God. This must be regarded as an assignment from God.

The apostle Paul wrote a letter to Philemon concerning his spiritual son Onesimus who was once under the tutelage and in the service of Philemon:

> Therefore, though I have abundant boldness in Christ to charge you to do what is fitting and required and your duty to do, yet for love's sake I prefer to appeal to you just for what I am—I, Paul, an ambassador [of Christ Jesus] and an old man and now a prisoner for His sake also—I appeal to you for my [own spiritual] child, Onesimus [meaning profitable], whom I have begotten [in the faith] while a captive in these chains.
>
> Once he was unprofitable to you, but now he is indeed profitable to you as well as to me.
>
> I am sending him back to you in his own person, [and it is like sending] my very heart.
>
> I would have chosen to keep him with me, in order that he might minister to my needs in your stead during my imprisonment for the Gospel's sake.
>
> But it has been my wish to do nothing about it without first consulting you and getting your consent, in order that your benevolence might not seem to be the result of compulsion or of pressure but might be voluntary [on your part].
>
> Perhaps it was for this reason that he was separated [from you] for a while, that you might have him back as yours forever, not as a slave any longer but as [something] more than a slave, as a brother [Christian], especially dear to me but how much more to you, both in the flesh [as a servant] and in the Lord [as a fellow believer].
>
> If then you consider me a partner and a comrade in fellowship, welcome and receive him as you would [welcome and receive] me.
>
> And if he has done you any wrong in any way or owes anything [to you], charge that to my account.
>
> I, Paul, write it with my own hand, I promise to repay it [in full]— and that is to say nothing [of the fact] that you owe me your very self!
>
> —PHILEMON 8–19

Satan retaliates against the order of God in the home, and will work through governmental systems of authority to separate men from their seed. When the children of Israel were in Egypt, Pharaoh put a plan into operation that would have eliminated the male Hebrew babies as their mothers were giving birth to them. It was a directive that came from the highest level of governmental authority in the nation.

> Then the king of Egypt said to the Hebrew midwives, of whom one was named Shiprah and the other Puah, when you act as midwives to the Hebrew women and see them on the birthstool, if it is a son, you shall kill him; but if it is a daughter, she shall live.
> But the midwives feared God and did not do as the king of Egypt commanded, but let the male babies live.
> —EXODUS 1:15–17

Satan still works through governmental agencies and systems to separate fathers from society and their children. It is through the judicial system that people, who are imprisoned by Satan in the spirit, are imprisoned by a system in the natural. This governmental system is in place to maintain law and order for the protection of its citizens and for the apprehension and retention of willful and habitual career criminals. But Satan also uses this system to his advantage to separate children from their fathers. His strategy is to take the father out of the home. Then he puts his plan into operation to capture the children and use them to his advantage because they are unprotected by the male.

Mankind is sinful because he was born with a sinful nature. He is lawless and disobedient because of the power of sin and Satan in his life. Satan uses fathers as drug lords, criminals, petty thieves, rapists, and assassins to carry out his acts of violence, murder, and destruction against the family of mankind. As the system incarcerates fathers and they are withdrawn from the life of their children, women, grandparents, or even foster parents have had to take responsibility of these headless households and parentless children.

Where there is no spiritual covering, children are easy prey for the devil. When the child reaches a certain stage of maturity, the devil begins his attack by releasing spirits of rebellion and lawlessness against children. They become antagonistic and indifferent toward all forms of authority and discipline.

At the age of puberty, sons need good fathers to be actively involved in their lives. In households where the father has abandoned his position and the son is lost for lack of fatherly wisdom, counsel, and direction, that son can become defiant, angry, lawless, difficult to deal with, and disobedient, leaving his mother overwhelmed, exasperated, disgusted, and frustrated.

The church has to understand this strategy of the enemy against the family and assume the responsibility of filling the void by raising up spiritual fathers and wise men who can give direction and counsel to the present generation of fatherless children.

Abraham was a father, Isaac was a father, and Jacob was a father. All the patriarchs were known as fathers, and in their generation they taught their children about the true and living God. Throughout the generations of the children of Israel, the people knew God as the God of Abraham, Isaac and Jacob.

There is a need in the body of Christ for men with the ministry of a father—men who would take another man's spiritual or natural seed that was abandoned and rejected and mentor that seed with the love of God, having compassion, correcting, reproving, cherishing, nourishing, and imparting godly wisdom. When men like Joseph stand before God, they will get their reward for being a father.

> Behold, I will send you Elijah the prophet before the great and terrible day of the Lord comes.
>
> And he shall turn and reconcile the hearts of the [estranged] fathers to the [ungodly] children, and the hearts of the [rebellious] children to [the piety of] their fathers [a reconciliation produced by repentance of the ungodly], lest I come and smite the land with a curse and a ban of utter destruction.
>
> —MALACHI 4:5–6

THE FATHER'S HONOR

A son honors his father, and a servant his master. If then I am a Father, where is My honor? And if I am a Master, where is the [reverent] fear due Me? says the Lord of hosts to you, O priests, who despise My name. You say, How and in what way have we despised Your name?
—MALACHI 1:6

Honor

In the above text honor denotes high regard or great respect, high rank or position, distinction, dignity, to be regarded highly, to show great respect, to treat with deference and courtesy, to worship.

It is a title of respect given to certain officials, for example:

Your Honor is a term used to address judges. *Your Majesty* is a term used to address kings or queens. *Your Excellency* is a term used to address dignitaries such as presidents.

> And the LORD said unto Moses, Take thee Joshua the son of Nun, a man in whom is the spirit, and lay thine hand upon him; and set him before Eleazar the priest, and before all the congregation; and give him a charge in their sight.
>
> And thou shalt put some of thine honour upon him, that all the congregation of the children of Israel may be obedient.
>
> —NUMBERS 27:18–20, KJV

> Regard (treat with honor, due obedience, and courtesy) your father and mother, that your days may be long in the land the Lord your God gives you.
>
> —EXODUS 20:12

Not only must honor be given to our natural parents but our spiritual parents must be held in high regard also. As we read the Old Testament, we will observe the high honor and respect given to fathers. The patriarchs (the ancient fathers) taught us a very important principle: the obligation of the fathers to bless their children before their death and speak prophetically into their life concerning their destiny.

This was not just an Old Testament principle, but Jesus practiced this principle before His departure. On the day of His departure back to the Father, Jesus took His disciples, His spiritual sons, out as far as Bethany. He gave them instructions, and He blessed them. While He was doing so, He was taken up from them in a cloud.

We do not know the exact words Jesus used to bless His disciples, but He taught us that fathers can decree and declare words of blessing into the lives of their children and God would honor the father's word. Fathers not only have the ability to mentor and protect the gift within their children, but they also have the authority to decree and release the blessings of God to their children who are in business and ministry.

Fathers can also decree evil. A father can curse his children like Jacob cursed his oldest son Reuben. Reuben had disrespected, disgraced, and embarrassed his father by having intercourse with his father's concubine Bilhah on his father's bed. Jacob never forgave Reuben. He cursed him instead of blessing him, and Reuben lost the status and the blessings of the firstborn son. Those things were given to Joseph.

> And Jacob called for his sons and said, Gather yourselves together [around me], that I may tell you what shall befall you in the latter or last days.
>
> Gather yourselves together and hear, you sons of Jacob; and hearken to Israel your father.
>
> Reuben, you are my firstborn, my might, the beginning (the firstfruits) of my manly strength and vigor; [your birthright gave you] the preeminence in dignity and the preeminence in power.
>
> But unstable and boiling over like water, you shall not excel and have the preeminence [of the firstborn], because you went to your father's bed; you defiled it—he went to my couch!
>
> —GENESIS 49:1–4

Isaac Blesses Jacob

> May God Almighty bless you and make you fruitful and multiply you until you become a group of peoples.
>
> May He give the blessing [He gave to] Abraham to you and your descendants with you, that you may inherit the land He gave to Abraham, in which you are a sojourner.
>
> —GENESIS 28:3–4

> And may God give you of the dew of the heavens and of the fatness of the earth and abundance of grain and [new] wine; let peoples serve you and nations bow down to you; be master over your brothers, and let your mother's sons bow down to you. Let everyone be cursed who curses you and favored with blessings who blesses you.
>
> —GENESIS 27:28–29

Jacob Blesses Joseph

And he blessed Joseph, and said:

"God, before whom my fathers Abraham and Isaac walked, the God who has fed me all my life long to this day, the Angel who has redeemed me from all evil, bless the lads; let my name be named upon them, and the name of my fathers Abraham and Isaac; and let them grow into a multitude in the midst of the earth."

—Genesis 48:15–16, nkjv

Joseph is a fruitful bough, a fruitful bough by a well (spring or fountain), whose branches run over the wall.

Skilled archers have bitterly attacked and sorely worried him; they have shot at him and persecuted him.

But his bow remained strong and steady and rested in the Strength that does not fail him, for the arms of his hands were made strong and active by the hands of the Mighty God of Jacob, by the name of the Shepherd, the Rock of Israel, by the God of your father, Who will help you, and by the Almighty, Who will bless you with blessings of the heavens above, blessings lying in the deep beneath, blessings of the breasts and of the womb.

The blessings of your father [on you] are greater than the blessings of my forefathers [Abraham and Isaac on me] and are as lasting as the bounties of the eternal hills; they shall be on the head of Joseph, and on the crown of the head of him who was the consecrated one and the one separated from his brethren and [the one who] is prince among them.

—Genesis 49:22–26

Love: The Greatest Gift of Fathers

But I want you to know and realize that Christ is the Head of every man, the head of a woman is her husband, and the Head of Christ is God.

—1 Corinthians 11:3

In the realm of the spirit, the kingdom of heaven is the sovereign kingdom that rules over all. Man is next in rank in the material world, which is the kingdom of man. Man is divided into male and female. The order in the kingdom of man according to covering and rank is first the male, then the female. The head of every married woman is her husband, but if a woman is single or is a widow, her father or older brother becomes her covering.

There is rank and order in the kingdom of heaven. First, there is God the Father. Seated at His right hand of authority is His Son Jesus Christ. Next in line is the Holy Spirit in all His sevenfold manifestations.

Out of man God brought forth the woman, and out of the relationship between the man and the woman children are born. This unit is called a family or a household, which is identified or recognized by the name of the man who is the head of the household. Every male child born into that family bears the name of the father and carries that name into the generations that follow. However, when the female marries, she covenants with her husband and carries his name or the name of his family. If she divorces and remarries ten times, each time she remarries her name changes so that she can be identified as the wife of her current husband.

The admonition given to the man was, "Husbands, love your wives, as Christ loved the church and gave Himself up for her.... Even so husbands should love their wives as [being in a sense] their own bodies. He who loves his own wife loves himself" (Eph. 5:25, 28).

Love is the greatest gift a man can bestow on his family. A real man of God is someone who knows how to walk in love. God is a Father, and God is love. Love is all about giving of oneself. When we give ourselves unselfishly in our marriage relationship, we honor the character of God. Giving out of love is choosing to be like God. God loves us because God is love, and to prove it, He gave the world the most precious thing that He had, His only Son. What father do you know would give his only son to die for the world?

The love of God compels giving. This kind of love is the foundation on which you build a marriage relationship. It positions you to have a prosperous marriage.

> God so loved the world that He gave His only begotten Son, that whoever believes in Him should not perish but have everlasting life.
> —JOHN 3:16, NKJV

There is a difference between love and lust. Love gives; lust takes. A luster is satisfied to have sex with a woman outside of marriage because lust does not want to be committed and is afraid of responsibility. A lover and a luster may go after the same thing, but the difference with love is that love endures.

Lust is selfish; lust is impatient. Lust may start off doing the same things as love, but eventually lust stops after it has achieved its goal. Lust does not take responsibility for the problems it has conceived. Lust is anything desired in a selfish, unloving way. There is nothing to hold a marriage together that is based on lust. Lust is always looking for a return on the measure that it gives, and if it takes too long to manifest, lust changes its position. Lust is covetous; a luster will stay in a relationship with you as long as that relationship is beneficial to the luster.

Jesus gave us an illustration in Matthew 7 that can be used to describe the household of the luster and the household of the lover. There were two men who were builders, and each man built a house. One built his house on a rock, and the other built his house on the sand. When the rains descended, the floods came. The winds blew and beat upon each house. The house that was built upon a rock, an unshakeable foundation, stood strong against the elements and withstood the shaking, the torrents, and the hostile forces of nature. But the one that was built upon the sand could not withstand the pressures that came against it, so it fell.

Love is an unshakable foundation. Love covers a multitude of sins. Strong love kept one man's house from falling apart when the same tragedies struck and demolished another man's household.

Love is a bond that holds people together in relationship and fellowship. Jesus gave the church a new commandment that states, "Love the Lord your God with all your heart….and love your neighbor as [you do] yourself" (Matt. 22:37, 39). Love is a quality and the character of God.

> Love endures long and is patient and kind; love never is envious nor boils over with jealousy, is not boastful or vainglorious, does not display itself haughtily.
>
> It is not conceited (arrogant and inflated with pride); it is not rude (unmannerly) and does not act unbecomingly. Love (God's love in us) does not insist on its own rights or its own way, for it is not self-seeking; it is not touchy or fretful or resentful; it takes no account of the evil done to it [it pays no attention to a suffered wrong].
>
> It does not rejoice at injustice and unrighteousness, but rejoices when right and truth prevail.

Love bears up under anything and everything that comes, is ever ready to believe the best of every person, its hopes are fadeless under all circumstances, and it endures everything [without weakening].

Love never fails [never fades out or becomes obsolete or comes to an end]. As for prophecy (the gift of interpreting the divine will and purpose), it will be fulfilled and pass away; as for tongues, they will be destroyed and cease; as for knowledge, it will pass away [it will lose its value and be superseded by truth].

—1 Corinthians 13:4–8

When a marriage relationship has been impacted by lust, it opens the door for abuse, disrespect, unfaithfulness, and the alienation of affection. Lust promotes hopelessness, resentment, fear, unforgiveness, and lack of trust by the affected spouse, especially if there is no remorse or a lack of repentance by the offending spouse. This causes the relationship to lose its potential to survive. It loses it's savor and sweetness. Salt is not salt if it loses its savor; sugar is not sugar if it loses its sweetness. In the same way, marriage cannot be a divine institution without love.

This state of disharmony cancels the power of agreement, making it void and ineffective because it alienates the soul from the primary ingredient that makes marriage a union of the heart and soul.

What happens to a marriage relationship when brokenness, anger, and bitterness has taken root in the heart? The relationship begins to malfunction. What happens to a relationship when a woman no longer has the desire (love) and craving in her flesh for her husband? She loses her desire to have sex with him.

To the woman He said, I will greatly multiply your grief and your suffering in pregnancy and the pangs of childbearing; with spasms of distress you will bring forth children. Yet your desire and craving will be for your husband, and he will rule over you.

—Genesis 3:16

A husband cannot rule over a woman who has no desire or craving for him unless he rules by force. If he is ruling his household with an iron hand, every sexual encounter with his wife will be a forced encounter or sexual battery. To have nonconsensual sex with a woman who has no desire for you is called rape, an encounter that is void of love or passion. There is no true worship in that type of sexual encounter. When a husband stops being a lover and becomes a boss or a tyrant in the home, he is no longer a worshiper. It is the power of agreement that brings the man and his wife together in the act of worship. Their passion and desire engages them in consensual sex in the bond of love and unity. It is in this harmonious union where God is in the midst.

There is nothing in the scripture that gives us the interpretation that the man, in his capacity as head of the family, is a boss. When a man sees himself as a boss, a tyrant or dictator over his family, that depiction changes the dynamics of the relationship because it cancels out the words *love* and *cherish*. If he is stubborn and indifferent and does not listen to any suggestions from his wife or children, discussions and family conversations become nonexistent because he will cast their words to the ground because in his mind, he thinks that his wife is inferior to him and she cannot minister to him.

Though there may be physical, emotional, and psychological differences between the male and the female, together they complete and enhance each other by forming a unit, each dependent on the other. God holds the man ultimately responsible for the household that comes into being through the marriage. Husbands have, at times, thought this responsibility gives them special privileges that allow them to treat their wives with disdain instead of as equals, but such a state of affairs was not God's original intention. Both the husband and wife must exercise submission to one another. When a husband lacks good character and the love of God, his ego and pride may cause him to verbally, physically, emotionally, or mentally abuse his family.

Women fall into various groups depending on the personality type. Culture, values, mind-sets, and predisposition play a role in determining behavior and personality. Some women may be passive and easy to control. Some, because of prior abuse and victimization, may have a victim's mentality or a vindictive personality. Some may be immature for their age, and some may be mentally, morally, or spiritually weak. Others may have strong personalities and a dominant spirit; they know how to take control of the home if the husband is inept. Some are good managers and can provide and manage the household if the husband has abandoned the home. Some women are wise, ambitious, educated, and know what they want out of life and relationships, and they complement their husbands. They make good marriage and business partners.

Then, there are those women who are manipulative, controlling, judgmental, cunning, and crafty, who cannot receive correction but they make demands and love to correct others. This type of woman is loud and stubborn, and her spirit is out of control. Others are brave and courageous, spiritually mature, because they have a seasoned relationship with God. Then there are those strong women with the spirit of a warrior. She is combative. She will not take any nonsense from anybody, she will not be a victim, she will not be manipulated, she will not be cheated on, she will not be lied to, she will fight to maintain her position with every weapon at her disposal, and she will be respected.

If the atmosphere in the home is one of constant friction, fighting, arguments, cursing, and abuse, it will produce a climate in which spirits of disharmony, strife, division, anger, and rebellion, among other things, will subtly take residence in the home. This will eventually set the stage for divorce.

Sin has spoiled the marriage relationship as it has spoiled everything else in human society. However, because of the exercise of agape love, Christian marriages ought to achieve a state of marital harmony, where the man and his wife practice forgiveness. Since our relationship with Christ governs the marriage relationship, the Christian should do everything possible to make the marriage work in harmony, as the apostle Paul admonished husbands to love their wives as Christ loves the church.

Some years ago, I was invited to a home to minister to a family. As I entered the home, the Holy Spirit whispered to me, "Ephesians 5." As we gathered for prayer and the reading of the Word, I used that scripture as my text. It opened a can of worms. The wife and husband had been fighting over finances for years, each one accusing the other partner for the lack of cohesiveness in the home, but neither of them listened to the complaints expressed by the other. They had no common ground for any harmonious discussions, just disgust, disrespect, strife, bitterness, and anger.

The wife was disgusted and frustrated with her husband because he would not listen to her complaints, so she fussed and complained. She was carrying the financial weight of the family, they were having too many babies, she was tired with the demands on her job and family, and she wanted to take some time off to rest and to bring some structure into the lives of the children, who were falling behind in school.

The husband, on the other hand, just ignored his wife and stayed away from home as often and as long as he could. His plan was to save enough of his money to buy a new car, which could not happen if the wife took a leave of absence from her job because he could not make up for the loss of income. There was no plan in place. No one listened, and the fight kept escalating until the Holy Spirit intervened.

Women and men approach a relationship with a different frame of mind because physiologically they are different. Most men avoid commitment to a marriage covenant because they see themselves trapped in a relationship with one woman. But the majority of men think love and sex are one and the same. If he has a physical dysfunction and cannot function sexually, he looses interest in other aspects of showing affection like embracing, caressing, kissing, etc., because in his mind he cannot take it to the other level.

Women, on the other hand, want to belong. She wants a man to commit to her, and she embraces commitment and faithfulness in the bond of marriage. She will use sex as a device to trap a man because of the weakness of his flesh.

For women, marriage is comprised of an entire package, and sex is a part of that package. However, a married woman wants to be caressed and appreciated above and beyond sex. For her, love is spending quality time with each other, caring about each other's needs, giving moral support, verbalizing your appreciation, keeping the element of surprise in the relationship, lending assistance that will relieve stress, listening, hugging, defending, complimenting, blessing, and working together to attain stated goals. Sex in marriage is the result of all of the above, and all of these elements working together make marriage fun and enjoyable.

In return, the woman honors her husband and craves his attention, and her desire is always to please him. In the Old Testament, Sarah called her husband, Abraham, "lord," because she honored him, acknowledged his status, and respected his relationship with God. Abraham was considered as lord among his peers because he was a man of great wealth, which gave him rank and status in his community as an elder statesman. He was a chief among the men in his region. Great men like Abimelech, the king of the Philistines, and Pharaoh, king of Egypt, gave Abraham gifts of money, cattle, and servants.

Abraham provided for his entire household of over three hundred eighteen servants. (See Genesis 14:14.) They also called him "lord" because he was their master. Many of these servants were born while their parents worked in the employ of Abraham and lived in his household, and they called Abraham "father" because he provided for them.

It was thus that Sarah obeyed Abraham [following his guidance and acknowledging his headship over her by] calling him lord (master, leader, authority). And you are now her true daughters if you do right and let nothing terrify you [not giving way to hysterical fears or letting anxieties unnerve you].

In the same way you married men should live considerately with [your wives], with an intelligent recognition [of the marriage relation], honoring the woman as [physically] the weaker, but [realizing that you] are joint heirs of the grace (God's unmerited favor) of life, in order that your prayers may not be hindered and cut off. [Otherwise you cannot pray effectively.]

—1 PETER 3:6–7

Sarah eventually gave birth to her only son Isaac. Isaac was Abraham's heir, the promised son, but Isaac had a different disposition and temperament than his father. He inherited his father's enormous wealth, but he was pampered by his mother. He did not have to struggle for anything in his life, all his needs were met, but Isaac needed a wife who would complement him, a wife who was going in the same prophetic direction as he was. His father did not want him to marry outside of his realm or status, therefore, Abraham arranged for his son's marriage to Rebekah.

The most important part of marriage is making the right choice in partnership. Women choose with their heart, and some of them are blinded by their infatuation with the outward appearance of a man, loving what he looks like and not taking heed to the warning signs. These women seldom take the aspects of a man's character into consideration.

The right partner can enhance you, and the wrong partner can bring shame, regrets, abuse, disappointment, and sometimes even premature death. Many young women whose family members never had a history of criminal activity found themselves in trouble with the law because of their relationship with men involved in criminal activity.

As a father, Abraham was involved in the choice of his son's wife because Rebekah had much to inherit by marrying his son Isaac. Abraham, being a wise father, did not want his inheritance to fall in the wrong hands or to be squandered by the wrong people. A good father leaves an inheritance to his children's children, and Abraham's wealth was a blessing to be passed on to the generations to come.

One of the primary virtues a loving father and husband must have is wisdom. The wisdom of God is of paramount importance if direction must come from the head. The head is the savior of the body. The word *savior* in this sentence denotes protector, shield, and covering. The head gives direction to the body, which is why Jesus Christ is the head of the church.

The Garden of Eden was the place where the devil launched his first attack against the institution of marriage, the family, the power of agreement, and truth. His plan was to intercept the relationship between God and mankind. His strategy was to divide and conquer; this resulted in a permanent disconnection between the mind of God and the mind of man. Man would no longer be on the same frequency with heaven.

After the fall of man, Satan set up his headquarters in the second heaven, a strategic position between the third heaven (God's throne) and the earth (man's domain). Any transmissions between the thoughts of God and the mind of man were intercepted, and Satan began infiltrating the man's mind with his sadistic, ungodly thoughts and fantasies, which affected man's behavior and lifestyle. His plan was to destroy the relationship between God and man, to keep man out of the presence of God, to deface the image and likeness of God in man, and to pollute man's holy nature so that man would no longer act like God or have godly instincts and character.

Satan launched an indirect attack against the man by attacking the woman, but Satan's primary target was the man who God instituted as head of the family and head of the human race, because he was created first. The woman came out of the man, and children come out of the union of the man and the woman.

Headship is a position of authority and leadership. After the fall of the first Adam, God sent His Son Jesus Christ into the earth as the second Adam to fulfill the mandate He gave to the first Adam. He was responsible for replenishing the earth with a generation of children who were, according to the law of generation, in the image and likeness of their Father, as Adam was the image and likeness of God. The law of generation states that every seed must produce after its kind.

The first Adam was created a living soul. The soul is the seat of man's personality, the mind, the will, and the intellect. Adam was the most intellectual man who ever lived. He knew and understood the power of the mind. He could conceive and perceive something in his mind and the force of his will could bring it into manifestation. Adam could travel to different places in the Garden of Eden by using the power of his thoughts, will, and mind.

Satan approached Eve as an intellectual being, a person given to reasoning and debate, and through the power of the mind and reasoning, he enticed her to question what God said, causing doubt to arise in her heart. When she acquiesced to his statements and tasted the fruit of the tree that God told them not to eat of, and gave to her husband, the word of God came to pass, for God said, "In the day that you eat of it you shall surely die" (Gen 2:17).

To undo the dead works of the first Adam, Jesus would pay the price justice demanded for Adam's sin and the curse that fell on his generation of children born of the corrupted seed of Adam.

Before the foundations of the world, God put in place a safety net for mankind. If man sinned, it was predetermined by God that Jesus, the second Adam, would die on a cross to pay the price of redemption for the human race, but as he hung on the cross, Satan orchestrated an attack when a soldier wounded him by piercing his side with a sword. Out of this wound poured blood and water. His blood paid the price for the redemption of Adam's fallen generation, and the water is a cleansing agent for His bride, the church.

> Not by works of righteousness which we have done, but according to His mercy He saved us, through the washing of regeneration and renewing of the Holy Spirit.
>
> —TITUS 3:5, NKJV

In attacking the woman, Satan was attacking the honor of the man. Wives are admonished to honor their husbands. The enemy observed her and took notice of her sensitivity, the nurturing aspect of her personality, her curiosity, her generosity, her passion, and her innocence. These are good qualities, but Satan pulled a weapon called deception out of his arsenal and launched a successful attack against the man's honor, his inheritance, possession, and dominion.

Then Adam, operating under the power of agreement, tasted of the fruit when his wife brought it to him, and because she ate it, he also ate. Together they lost their dominion status and were driven out of their kingdom inheritance, the Garden of Eden. Adam remained committed to his wife until death. We could blame the devil, but Adam made a decision to eat the fruit because he was in agreement with his wife until God showed up and Adam had to deal with the consequences of his disobedience. Adam blamed God for giving him the woman, and the woman blamed the serpent for their demise.

Satan and man have not changed their ways. The strategy Satan used in Eden is still being used today because it was an effective strategy. The spirit of deception is a weapon and a device that the devil and men still use against women. Men and women lie and cheat and still say, "I love you." The gullible, the ignorant, the uninformed, the innocent, the wayward, the lawless, and the rebellious are all victims of the spirit of deception. Women must be aware of this; deception is an area where women are most vulnerable.

Because of the incident in Eden, God said to the woman, "Your desire will be to your husband and he shall rule over you." (See Genesis 3:16.) That word released a supernatural bond or divine attachment that will always draw the wife to her husband, except in the case of abuse and unfaithfulness. Anytime a wife is left to fend for herself and to act independently of her husband, she attracts the spirit of deception. If she takes her car to be serviced, the spirit of deception is at the dealership or repair shop to see to it that she pays for work that was not done on her car. According to the law of first use, Satan is still using that weapon against the woman. Her husband is her first line of defense and is responsible to God to shield and defend his wife and to confront that lying spirit of deception.

As the marriage relationship matures and the man and his wife become one spiritually, physically, and emotionally, the wife, without realizing it, will always be desirous of being emotionally bonded and taking her place of comfort at his side where she belongs. This is the reason why in marriages that have lasted for many decades and the two have attained a state of oneness, when one spouse dies, the other spouse expires not too long after.

THE CURSE OF THE ILLEGITIMATE CHILD

> A person begotten out of wedlock shall not enter into the assembly of the Lord; even to his tenth generation shall his descendants not enter into the congregation of the Lord.
> —DEUTERONOMY 23:2

When God brought Israel out of Egypt, they became a nation under God by accepting the terms of the covenant prescribed by God, which stated that He would be their God and they would be His people. This made Israel a very peculiar people because all their laws, civil, moral and spiritual, were given to them by God. These laws were to govern their day-to-day lives and the worship of their God, Jehovah. God's plan was for Israel to be a kingdom of priests and a holy nation, and anyone who did not adhere to and give assent to the words of the Law to do them as the rule of his life was cursed by God. There were blessings for obedience and curses for rebellion.

> Now therefore, if you will obey My voice in truth and keep My covenant, then you shall be My own peculiar possession and treasure from among and above all peoples; for all the earth is Mine.
> And you shall be to Me a kingdom of priests, a holy nation [consecrated, set apart to the worship of God]. These are the words you shall speak to the Israelites.
> —EXODUS 19:5–6

This was a theocratic society, and breaking God's law was equivalent to breaking state or national laws in a democratic society. The difference was as Eli, the high priest, so rightly said:

> If one man wrongs another, God will mediate for him; but if a man wrongs the Lord, who shall intercede for him?
> —1 SAMUEL 2:25

One of the significant differences between the two systems of government was the justice system. A judicial system in a democratic society issues fines as a means of reciprocation and incarcerates lawbreakers to meet society's demands for punishment and justice. In a theocratic society, those who transgress God's laws were cursed, and the capital punishment for one found guilty of any heinous crimes was death by stoning.

Cursing in the ancient Hebrew world was not a burst of bad language as it usually is in the world of today. It was a pronouncement of judgment believed to bring the release of powerful spiritual forces against the person cursed. For this reason, it was as great a sin to curse a deaf person as it was to put a stumbling block in the path of a blind person. For the deaf person, not having heard the curse could not defend himself with the more powerful blessing of Yahweh.

The rewards to those who obeyed God's commandments are called blessings. The judgments upon those who disobey God's commandments are called curses. God's curse on people or things was more than a pronouncement of devastating judgment; it was a punishment for sin.

> Cursed is he who dishonors his father or his mother. All the people shall say, Amen.
>
> Cursed is he who moves [back] his neighbor's landmark. All the people shall say, Amen.
>
> Cursed is he who misleads a blind man on his way. All the people shall say, Amen.
>
> Cursed is he who perverts the justice due to the sojourner or the stranger, the fatherless, and the widow. All the people shall say, Amen.
>
> Cursed is he who lies with his father's wife, because he uncovers what belongs to his father. All the people shall say, Amen.
>
> Cursed is he who lies with any beast. All the people shall say, Amen.
>
> Cursed is he who lies with his half sister, whether his father's or his mother's daughter. All the people shall say, Amen.
>
> Cursed is he who lies with his mother-in-law. All the people shall say, Amen.
>
> Cursed is he who slays his neighbor secretly. All the people shall say, Amen.
>
> Cursed is he who takes a bribe to slay an innocent person. All the people shall say, Amen.
>
> Cursed is he who does not support and give assent to the words of this law to do them [as the rule of his life]. All the people shall say, Amen.
>
> —Deuteronomy 27:16–26

The Origin of Curses

Curses originated from God. The first curse we have on record that was levied by God was to the serpent, the woman, and to the earth because of the temptation and subsequent fall of man in the Garden of Eden. God gave this right and privilege to the priestly tribe of Levi, to tribal leaders, judges, and persons in authority.

> And the Lord God said to the serpent, Because you have done this, you are cursed above all [domestic] animals and above every [wild]

living thing of the field; upon your belly you shall go, and you shall eat dust [and what it contains] all the days of your life.

To the woman He said, I will greatly multiply your grief and your suffering in pregnancy and the pangs of childbearing; with spasms of distress you will bring forth children. Yet your desire and craving will be for your husband, and he will rule over you.

And to Adam He said, Because you have listened and given heed to the voice of your wife and have eaten of the tree of which I commanded you, saying, You shall not eat of it, the ground is under a curse because of you; in sorrow and toil shall you eat [of the fruits] of it all the days of your life.

—Genesis 3:14, 16–17

When Adam's son Cain murdered his brother, Abel, a curse was released against Cain because Cain shed the blood of another human being. The life of a man is in the blood. Only God deserves the right to take the life of a man, because He gave man life. Cain was the first murderer, the first man to shed the blood of another man, and he was cursed. Subsequently, according to the law of first use, all murderers are cursed people.

And the Lord said to Cain, Where is Abel your brother? And he said, I do not know. Am I my brother's keeper?

And [the Lord] said, What have you done? The voice of your brother's blood is crying to Me from the ground.

And now you are cursed by reason of the earth, which has opened its mouth to receive your brother's [shed] blood from your hand.

—Genesis 4:9–11

There were different curses for various offenses, but disobedience to any of God's law resulted in judgment. As the nation of God, Israel had laws that dictated that a man was not supposed to touch a woman before they were married. This law was a part of the culture of that society. All young brides, with the exception of widows, had to be virgins when they were married. To lose one's virginity before marriage brought shame and reproach to the young woman and her family. The legitimacy of the marriage covenant was based on the woman being a virgin. This was a part of the tradition, especially in that society where the marriage was often arranged by the parents. Out of the purity of the marriage bed the blessings of God were manifested, and the fruit of the womb was God's reward.

> There shall be no whore of the daughters of Israel, nor a sodomite of the sons of Israel.
>
> —Deuteronomy 23:17, kjv

> Now Dinah daughter of Leah, whom she bore to Jacob, went out [unattended] to see the girls of the place.
>
> And when Shechem son of Hamor the Hivite, prince of the country, saw her, he seized her, lay with her, and humbled, defiled, and disgraced her.
>
> But his soul longed for and clung to Dinah daughter of Jacob, and he loved the girl and spoke comfortingly to her young heart's wishes.
>
> And Shechem said to his father Hamor, Get me this girl to be my wife.
>
> Jacob heard that [Shechem] had defiled Dinah his daughter. Now his sons were with his livestock in the field. So Jacob held his peace until they came.
>
> But Hamor father of Shechem went out to Jacob to have a talk with him.
>
> When Jacob's sons heard it, they came from the field; and they were distressed and grieved and very angry, for [Shechem] had done a vile thing to Israel in lying with Jacob's daughter, which ought not to be done.
>
> —Genesis 34:1–7

Among the heathen nations of that time, rape and incest was prevalent. Young women and young men had to be protected by the family. They could not be adventurous like Dinah, Jacob's daughter, who wandered away from the protection of the tribe, because they would be victims of rape or taken into captivity. Therefore, God gave the nation of Israel laws that would protect young girls and boys from this type of violation. But many of God's people violated these laws because of the inherently sinful nature of man. Israelite men adopted many of the practices of the heathen nations, one of which was that they had many wives and concubines (mistresses). These concubines gave birth to children out of wedlock, and many of these children were not given any inheritance by their fathers and had to find their own way in life. Upon the death of their father, they were left out of the distribution of the wealth of the family, for they were considered illegitimate, cursed children.

> Now Gideon had seventy sons born to him, for he had many wives.
>
> And his concubine, who was in Shechem, also bore him a son, whom he named Abimelech.
>
> Gideon son of Joash died at a good old age and was buried in the tomb of Joash his father in Ophrah of the Abiezrites.
>
> —Judges 8:30–32

> Now Abimelech son of Jerubbaal (Gideon) went to Shechem to his mother's kinsmen and said to them and to the whole clan of his mother's family, say, I pray you, in the hearing of all the men of Shechem, Which is better for you: that all seventy of the sons of Jerubbaal reign over you, or that one man rule over you? Remember also that I am your bone and your flesh.
>
> And his mother's kinsmen spoke all these words concerning him in the hearing of all the men of Shechem, and their hearts inclined to follow Abimelech, for they said, He is our brother.
>
> And they gave him seventy pieces of silver out of the house of Baal-berith, with which Abimelech hired worthless and foolhardy men who followed him.
>
> And he went to his father's house at Ophrah and slew his brothers the sons of Jerubbaal, seventy men, on one stone. But Jotham, the youngest son of Jerubbaal, was left, for he hid himself.
>
> —Judges 9:1–5

Many people's lives are totally inhibited because of the curse of the illegitimate child. Some of the traits of this curse are rebellion, witchcraft (manipulation, intimidation, control, seduction), poverty, waywardness, gang warfare, imprisonment, sexually transmitted diseases, criminal activity, alcoholism, brutality, murder, violence, promiscuity, weak-mindedness, hate, physical problems, sexual sins, premature death, illegitimate authority, rape, incest, drugs, mental breakdown (which migrates to other illness without clear medical diagnosis), miscarriages in pregnancy for women, and for men it is the miscarriage of vision, dreams, or occupations. Other symptoms are general family breakdown of marriage and alienation (when families become estranged from each other), being accident prone, unreasonable bad behavior, bad attitudes, and continued financial insufficiency.

Without a father's love and care, the curse of the illegitimate child manifests at an early age or when a child reaches the age of puberty. Rebellion against authority is the first manifestation of that curse. When lawlessness takes root in their heart, they defy authority figures, they curse their parents and their teachers, they refuse to take instructions, and many are nonachievers in school and go on to be nonachievers in life. Many young women, without the proper home environment, are pregnant before they graduate from high school or soon thereafter. They are also prone to drugs, alcohol, slander, distorting the truth, confusion, imprisonment, and a promiscuous lifestyle.

The curses produced in the life of these children block the release of the blessings of God. There are sicknesses that come with this curse, such as, physical and spiritual myopia, generational diseases, and familiar spirits. The curse of the illegitimate child put claims on people's business, their marriage, their ministry, their finances, and their children. Victimization can take place on the job because of the curse of the illegitimate child, where a person can do all the hard work and someone else gets the credit or the promotion.

The curse on men causes them to be irresponsible, unwilling to work, and to prefer to live at home with their mother or to live out of wedlock with their girlfriends. They avoid financial responsibility, they hustle women for money, they sell drugs, and they hunt like creatures of the night. They are involved in criminal activity, drugs, and alcoholism. They father children and refuse to pay child support.

The curse of the illegitimate child also prevents women from getting married but will permit them to cohabit with men and give birth to children with different fathers. It is not uncommon to see the women in certain families with children, yet there are no husbands. And if any of them should get married, after a while the marriage ends in divorce. Some of these women are drawn to have relationships only with married men, not understanding they are living out the curse they inherited from their mother.

The curse of the illegitimate child also fosters the spirit of homosexuality, rejection, sexual perversion, low self-esteem, and harlotry. It produces division and strife among family members and causes splits within churches.

King David, a chosen man of God, had sex with the wife of one of his trusted and loyal men, Uriah. Then David orchestrated the death of Uriah when he learned that Uriah's wife was pregnant by him. Even though David fasted and prayed, the baby was born and died in seven days because of the curse. This action of David displeased God, and God emitted a curse on David's household that the sword would not depart from David's house.

Even though David was a gifted psalmist, a gift never supersedes the authority or laws of God. His Word is anointed and is the sword of the Spirit. From an illicit affair with another man's wife, David produced an illegitimate child as an offspring, and the child died. As the leader of God's people, David was not an example to those around him. The prophet told David that he had given great occasion for the enemies of God to blaspheme God (2 Sam. 12:14). David paid a heavy price for his wrongdoing because the curse never left David's house. It manifested in his household as rape, murder, rejection, rebellion, and an attempted coup to drive him from his throne, led by his son Absalom.

> One evening David arose from his couch and was walking on the roof of the king's house, when from there he saw a woman bathing; and she was very lovely to behold.
>
> David sent and inquired about the woman. One said, Is not this Bathsheba, the daughter of Eliam and the wife of Uriah the Hittite?
>
> And David sent messengers and took her. And she came in to him, and he lay with her—for she was purified from her uncleanness. Then she returned to her house.
>
> And the woman became pregnant and sent and told David, I am with child. . . .
>
> And he [David] wrote in the letter, Put Uriah in the front line of the heaviest fighting and withdraw from him, that he may be struck down and die. . . .
>
> When Uriah's wife heard that her husband was dead, she mourned for Uriah.
>
> And when the mourning was past, David sent and brought her to his house, and she became his wife and bore him a son. But the thing that David had done was evil in the sight of the Lord. . . .
>
> Then Nathan said to David, You are the man! Thus says the Lord, the God of Israel: I anointed you king of Israel, and I delivered you out of the hand of Saul. . . .
>
> Why have you despised the commandment of the Lord, doing evil in His sight? You have slain Uriah the Hittite with the sword and

have taken his wife to be your wife. You have murdered him with the sword of the Ammonites.

Now, therefore, the sword shall never depart from your house, because [you have not only despised My command, but] you have despised Me and have taken the wife of Uriah the Hittite to be your wife.

Thus says the Lord, Behold, I will raise up evil against you out of your own house; and I will take your wives before your eyes and give them to your neighbor, and he shall lie with your wives in the sight of this sun.

For you did it secretly, but I will do this thing before all Israel and before the sun.

—2 SAMUEL 11:2–5, 15, 26–27; 2:7, 9–12

This curse has also affected many called into the ministry who have been hurt and rejected by their church leadership and have not be validated in their calling. When a church has been founded without the proper spiritual authority, the leading of the Holy Spirit, and the required spiritual foundation, it is affected by the curse of the illegitimate child. All the offspring born from that ministry will be affected by the curse. The sons of the ministry will be spiritually dwarfed, blind (no revelation), spiritually inhibited (no deliverance), presumptuous, and rebellious like their spiritual father or mother.

Keep back Your servant also from presumptuous sins; let them not have dominion over me! Then shall I be blameless, and I shall be innocent and clear of great transgression.

—PSALM 19:13

In churches where the curse of the illegitimate child is prevalent, there is a lack of support for the mission or vision of the church. People are judgmental and lack love. There is much slander, gossip, backbiting, criticisms, evil decrees, warfare among members, and prejudice, all of which are symptoms of the curse. It is very difficult to achieve success where there is a lack of love, cohesiveness, and where the spirit of competitive jealousy and sabotage is present. This curse can only be broken through confession, repentance, forgiveness, and the finished work of Calvary.

For those who have fathered or mothered children out of wedlock only the anointing of God can tear down the stronghold of this curse and restore one born illegitimate to legitimacy through the new birth, as one born of God.

> Therefore, if anyone is in Christ, he is a new creation; the old has gone, the new has come!
>
> —2 CORINTHIANS 5:17, NIV

Jesus took all the curses of mankind upon Himself when He was nailed to the cross. As the Redeemer and Savior of mankind, Jesus tasted the punishment of death for all, because all had sinned and fallen short of the glory of God. Jesus became cursed for mankind to satisfy God's demand for justice because of man's willful disobedience to the laws of God.

> Christ purchased our freedom [redeeming us] from the curse (doom) of the Law [and its condemnation] by [Himself] becoming a curse for us, for it is written [in the Scriptures], Cursed is everyone who hangs on a tree (is crucified).
>
> —GALATIANS 3:13

STEPS TO PERSONAL DELIVERANCE

Acknowledge and confess the iniquities of your forefathers, if you have not done so already. Ask yourself if there is a pattern of sin and dead works in your family. What are your family's sins, bad habits, weaknesses, failures, or illnesses? Have any family members been involved with the occult, drugs, alcoholism, sexual sins, hate, murder, shedding the blood of the innocent (abortion, genocide), unforgiveness, and known generational iniquities? You must examine the life of your predecessors from the last four or five generations and ask God to forgive their outstanding sins, and break all curses that are affecting the bloodline. Then close the door of inheritance in the name of Jesus.

The evil fruit in your life came from somewhere; the roots may be in another generation. Ask the Holy Spirit to help you discern and discover the sins that are hidden, and then ask God for mercy and forgiveness to cleanse you for participating in your family's iniquities.

> If they shall confess their iniquity, and the iniquity of their fathers, with their trespass which they trespassed against me, and that also they have walked contrary unto me....Then will I remember my covenant

with Jacob, and also my covenant with Isaac, and also my covenant
with Abraham will I remember; and I will remember the land.
—Leviticus 26:40, 42, kjv

And the seed of Israel separated themselves from all strangers, and
stood and confessed their sins, and the iniquities of their fathers.
—Nehemiah 9:2, kjv

Forgive your forefathers of family iniquities that have caused you problems,
and guard against the victim's mentality. This is the only way to break the
cycle of iniquity for yourself and the next generation. If we do not forgive men
their trespasses, neither will our heavenly Father forgive us of our trespasses.

Pray for Release From Curses

- I loose myself from every curse and unprofitable covenant, in
  the name of Jesus.

- Let every evil attachment to my place of birth be disconnected,
  in the name of Jesus.

- I break every curse of family destruction and debilitation, in
  the name of Jesus.

- I cancel and nullify any future covenant made against my life,
  in the name of Jesus.

- I cancel every evil effect of curses and covenants, in the name
  of Jesus.

- Let the blood of Jesus wash away my name from the notebook
  of dark powers, in the name of Jesus. Amen.

Chapter 3

DEFINING THE NEED FOR COVERING

For the bed is shorter than that a man can stretch himself on it: and the covering narrower than that he can wrap himself in it.

—Isaiah 28:20, KJV

PERSON IN MINISTRY CAN BE UNEQUALLY YOKED TOGETHER WITH THE wrong covering. A covering ministry is one that a minister or ministry is in covenant with. That covering minister or ministry is one that is on a higher rung in the realm of the spirit, and can facilitate the move of God, the upgrading of the ministry, and the broadening of the platform for the ministries that are under their spiritual care. They are watchmen in the spirit and can speak prophetically into the destiny of the ministries they cover. If the bed is short and the covering is narrow, it means that the covering is inadequate or ineffective and subsequently cannot properly bring that ministry up to a higher level in the spirit, nor can the covering ministry provide the tools to upgrade that ministry.

Women called to the ministry and who pastor churches must be careful with their choice of a ministry covering and a husband. In all instances they must be guided by the Holy Spirit, no matter who comes courting. Being yoked with the wrong mate or wrong ministry covering has caused many women who should be preaching behind pulpits, evangelizing in their community, and serving in the kingdom of God, to be sitting in the pews in a stagnant, distracted, overwhelmed state because of issues with their husbands or with ministries where male ministers do not believe women are called by God to a ministry of the Word of God.

An unbelieving husband can open the door for the enemy, if he is unfaithful and uncommitted to the marriage. Every act of unfaithfulness against the marriage bed would be an indirect attack against the wife's calling. Obedience to God is more vital than our necessary food, therefore, it is very important that women yield to the will of God and are led of the Holy Spirit in choosing a husband and a ministry covering that is going in the same prophetic direction as she is.

What if the call comes after marriage and the husband, who may be a believer, is not in agreement? God recognizes headship and understands authority because He is the sovereign God whose kingdom rules over all. But when a woman is called into ministry and her husband is not in agreement, Satan can use her husband to hinder the plan of God for his wife. If she is sensitive to the leading of the Holy Spirit, she has to spend much time in prayer and fasting and quietness before God so that the hand of God can intervene in her circumstances and the sovereign will of God can be accomplished in her life.

We are living in an age in which women are making great strides in education, business, ministry, politics, and various other endeavors. God does not remove the summons, even if the husband is not in agreement, and the Holy Spirit will continue to reveal Himself to the one who has been called until that person responds. God has many ways of bringing a person into compliance with His will. If she continues to resist the will of God, the Holy Spirit then begins to probe into those unsurrendered areas of her life, systematically breaking down her resistance. God will use the idols of the heart, her unbelieving husband, and whatever circumstances He can use to bring a person to completely surrender to His will.

There is an anointing that comes with the call, and there are trials and tests that accompany the call because of the Spirit of God's grace and glory that rest upon the individual. No matter what kind of burden or yoke is placed by man upon a vessel that God has chosen, God has assured us through His Word that the yoke will be broken and destroyed because of the anointing.

> And it shall come to pass in that day, that his burden shall be taken away from off thy shoulder, and his yoke from off thy neck, and the yoke shall be destroyed because of the anointing.
> —ISAIAH 10:27, KJV

There are many women in ministry whose marriages ended in divorce because of the will of their husbands, which was in direct conflict with the will and call of God on the life of the wife. Some of them remarried, while some remained single and continued their work for the kingdom of God. Everyone has their proper gift, but women with unbelieving husbands and women without husbands must align themselves in ministry with effective headship gifts that can embrace and enhance the call of God on their lives and provide the necessary prayer cover and anointing that is required.

What are some of the qualifying marks a woman should look for in a spiritual covering?

- Only God can qualify and designate an individual to be a spiritual covering over another spiritual gift. Women should be led by the Holy Spirit before choosing a covering.

- A woman's covering should be able to assist her in extending her platform and enlarging the scope of her ministry.

- A woman's covering must be anointed, a person of integrity and prayer; he or she must be filled with godly wisdom, faith, boldness, and courage.

- A woman's covering must walk in divine revelation of the Word of God.

- A woman's covering must be an example in faith, love, spirit, and character.

- A woman's covering must have a greater measure of the grace of God as it pertains to their positioning in the ministry.

- A woman's covering must have a good reputation both inside and outside of the church.

- A woman's covering must definitely believe and accept that God calls women to preach the gospel and pastor churches.

The relationship between the man and his wife is an indication of the strength of the anointing resting on the covering. A woman should not be in covenant with a headship gift if he is a man that abuses his wife.

There are many predators behind pulpits and in ministry, masquerading as ministry gifts. The biblical descriptive term for them is *tares*. Tares are pretenders, imposters, liars, and thieves who mimic genuine men and women of God, speak deception into the life of unsuspecting people, and use them to build their own kingdom. These imposters (or other descriptive seducers) prey on the spiritually immature and unsuspecting women when there is no husband or father that they must give account to.

The single, divorced, or separated woman called into ministry must be sure that the spiritual covering she submits herself to is not a pseudo prophet, one who has a problem with his flesh or with covetousness. She must do as the Bible requires us to do—try the spirit. The measuring line is the Word of God, and the Holy Spirit is the Spirit of truth who guides us into all truth. If there is a check in your spirit and uncertainty in your heart, the Holy Spirit is sending a smoke signal, and where there is smoke there is sure to be strange fire.

Women Who Marry Unbelievers

Loneliness is a cry from a desolate heart for fellowship, relationship, nurturing, and love. There are many single Christian women who are lonely because they don't have a husband or the support of a loving family. There are also many married women who are lonely in their relationship with their spouse. Loneliness in marriage is simply alienation of affection. It happens when a spouse withdraws his or her affection and becomes detached mentally and emotionally from their partner, and this can happen for various reasons.

Our diverse personality types are based on our life experiences, points of reference, verbal or nonverbal instructions, associations, environment, and family normality or dysfunctions. These conditions shape our character, personality, response, behavior, and perceptions of life. What causes loneliness in marriage is a lack of communication, selfishness, unresolved issues, wrong expectations, and unforgiveness. Marriage is an institution where our individual efforts, achievements, and contributions can be used to develop, support, benefit, and enhance the relationship between family members, but there must be communication.

Single people fall into various categories: widows, widowers, divorced, never been married, and separated. Single people are not always lonely. It depends on many factors, including their age, health, and personality. An introvert is a personality type whose interest is more in himself or herself than in his or her environment or in other people. These people tend to be more often alone and can be noncommunicative. Whereas, an extrovert is a personality type whose interest is more in his environment and in other people than in himself. This person is active and expressive. These personality types would be active in social groups. They do volunteer work, associate with community groups, and run for political office. They mingle, fellowship, and socialize. They find mediums of expression and communication.

When we marry, our personality and character traits have a great bearing on the type of relationship we will have with our spouse. Men and women belong to the same species of created beings, but their perceptions, insight, intuition, and awareness can be quite different. Men are more logical and seem unable to show emotion. They are a little slower at understanding their feelings regarding things or their appraisal of others, but when they do decide something, they usually have logical reasons for their conclusions. Women, on the other hand, are more emotional and tend to be more intuitive and communicative. Both are fearfully and wonderfully made (Ps. 139:14), but there is a difference in their God-given functions, purpose, and contribution in the earth.

> Now the Lord God said, It is not good (sufficient, satisfactory) that the man should be alone; I will make him a helper meet (suitable, adapted, complementary) for him.
>
> —Genesis 2:18

There are many women serving in ministry in the body of Christ whose husbands do not have a relationship with Jesus Christ. Pastor Angie is one of them. She accepted her call to the ministry and began pastoring a small church. She was told by the governing board of elders that her husband must be ordained and serve with her as pastor. She knew he did not qualify, but she kept quiet about it. The board of elders was predominantly men whose policy advocated that the pastor be male, never discerned her husband's spirit. Everyone thought he was flamboyant and friendly. He attended church regularly and did support the church financially, but his position as copastor only gave him an environment to continue his philandering ways. Within a year, he left his wife and the church and began cohabiting with another woman. This affected the church, which dwindled down to less than half its size. It also was an embarrassment to his wife and the board of elders, who chose him to be copastor only because of their view toward women in ministry.

Another woman minister testified that her husband gave her an ultimatum. He said, "You can come with me to the bars and be my drinking buddy, or you can serve God and be a divorced woman." She chose God, and her husband divorced her. Story after story has been told about women with the call of God on their lives who had to choose who they were going to serve—a husband who did not want to submit to God or to the call of God on their life.

> I had to make a choice. Would I serve the man I loved, or the God I loved? I knew I couldn't serve God and live with Mister. No one will ever know the pain of dying like I know it, for I loved him more than I loved life itself. And for a time, I loved him even more than God. I finally told him I had to leave, for God had never released me from my original call. Not only did I live with him, I had to live with my conscience, and the conviction of the Holy Spirit was almost unbearable, I was tired of trying to justify myself.[1]
>
> —KATHRYN KUHLMAN

"From the moment she made that decision, Kathryn Kuhlman never wavered from answering the call on her life, never deviated from the path God had for her, and never saw "Mister," her husband, again. She bought a one-way ticket to Franklin, Pennsylvania, and never turned back.[2]

Kathryn was totally restored in her life with God. Though this was a difficult time for Kathryn, the blessings of God soon followed her. But the fate of her husband was uncertain. He simply dropped out of sight, not even contacting his family. According to his ex-wife, Jessie, it was years later that his brother, James Waltrip, sadly discovered that Burroughs Waltrip had eventually met his death in a California prison, convicted of stealing money from a woman."[3]

> My dear sisters in Christ, as you hear these words may the Spirit of Christ come upon you, and make you willing to do the work the Lord has assigned to you. It is high time for women to let their lights shine; to bring out their talents that have been hidden away rusting; and use them for the glory of God, and do with their might what their hands find to do, trusting God for strength, who has said, "I will never leave you." Let us not plead weakness; God will use the weak things of the world to confound the wise. We are sons and daughters of the Most High God. Should we not honor our high calling and do all we can to save those who sit in the valley and shadow of death? Did He not send Moses, Aaron, Miriam to be your leaders? Barak dared not meet the enemy unless Deborah led the army. The Lord raised up men, women, and children of His own choosing, Hannah, Hulda, Anna, Phoebe, Narcissus, Tryphena, Persis, Julia, the Marys and the sisters who co-

labored with the Apostle Paul. Is it less becoming for women to labor
in Christ's kingdom and vineyard now than it was then?[4]

—Maria Woodworth-Etter

"Maria Woodworth-Etter's life was marked with great persecution. There
were problems around every corner, not to mention the pressures that came
from leading such huge masses of people who were experiencing their first
manifestations of the Spirit. In addition to all of this, she was a woman in
ministry who was married to an unfaithful man.

While ministering in a controversial crusade in Oakland, California, Maria
found out about her husband, P. H. Woodworth's, infidelity. They separated,
and she chose to leave him, and after twenty-six years of marriage, in January
1891, they were divorced. In less than a year and a half, P. H. Woodworth
remarried and publicly slandered Maria's character and ministry. He died not
too long after on June 21, 1892, of typhoid fever."[5]

Many women who are called to the ministry would like to marry and have the
support and covering of a husband. A husband-and-wife team would have a better
effect in ministry. However, in desperation, many women are marrying men who
never had a relationship with the Lord before they met their ministering wife, or
these men were recently saved and not yet delivered from their selfishness, habits,
and a mentality that is opposed to the will and ways of God.

As in the case of Pastor Angie, the man was given a title and thrust into
a position of rank and authority in the church before Christ was formed in
him. A married man who does not know the Lord is not to be considered as
the spiritual covering for a church even if his wife is the pastor. His place is
husband, father, provider, and protector of his own household. As the pastor's
husband, he too needs to be under the authority and mentorship of a spiritual
father. When a novice is given spiritual authority prematurely, pride sets in, and
if there is no spiritual father to hold him accountable, pride opens the door for
competitive jealousy and rivalry between the man and his wife. In the Apostle
Paul's summation of the qualifications for bishops and deacons he said:

> He must not be a new convert, or he may [develop a beclouded and
> stupid state of mind] as the result of pride [be blinded by conceit, and]
> fall into the condemnation that the devil [once] did.

Furthermore, he must have a good reputation and be well thought of by those outside [the church], lest he become involved in slander and incur reproach and fall into the devil's trap.

In like manner the deacons [must be] worthy of respect, not shifty and double-talkers but sincere in what they say, not given to much wine, not greedy for base gain [craving wealth and resorting to ignoble and dishonest methods of getting it].

They must possess the mystic secret of the faith [Christian truth as hidden from ungodly men] with a clear conscience.

And let them also be tried and investigated and proved first; then, if they turn out to be above reproach, let them serve [as deacons].

—1 TIMOTHY 3:6–10

Under the Levitical priesthood, men became priest by virtue of their relationship with the bloodline of Levi, their ancestor. But under the new covenant, we are priests unto God based on our relationship with Jesus Christ, who is our eternal High Priest of the rank and order of Melchizedek. This order of divine priesthood is based on the power of Christ's endless life, through which we have our eternal inheritance as sons of God and are joint heirs with Jesus Christ.

A man who does not know the Lord provides covering for his household, his own flesh and blood. But, like Eli, an Old Testament pastor, the church still has the tendency to put family members in positions of rank and authority in the house of God, not taking into consideration whether their lifestyle is consistent with the Word of God. A title or position of honor in the church does not deliver a man from a lifestyle that in inconsistent with holiness and biblical truth. To have a relationship with Jesus Christ begins with repentance, deliverance, reconciliation, restoration, justification, redemption abiding in the Word of God, and the Spirit of Christ abiding in us—this is the salvation package. It is an experience called the new birth or the born-again experience. One can join a church and not be joined to the Lord Jesus Christ. When we are joined to the Lord by the new birth, we are given the Spirit of Christ. If we do not have the Spirit of Christ, we do not belong to Christ.

If women in ministry marry men who do not know the Lord, then they are unequally yoked with an unbeliever. They must realize that their husband must first accept Christ as Lord and Savior, after which Christ has to be formed in him; which is a work of transformation, sanctification, and restoration. He must have a prayer life because prayer establishes communication with God. This is more important than a title or priestly service in the house of God.

Female pastors who married men who are spiritually immature should not allow their husbands to take on the responsibility of headship in the house of God prematurely; there should be a period of growth and development. It takes time for a professional to become an expert in his profession. No one can just put up a sign and presumptuously claim to be a doctor of medicine and invite people to come in for patient care when the person never took the time to be qualified and trained. To take on responsibilities involving the lives and destinies of people because of gender, without being qualified and trained, is presumption, and the results of this presumption can be detrimental to the people who respect and trust the advice and office of the leader.

Life is all about choices, and the choices we make as leaders, no matter how personal those choices are, can affect the community of people we are leading, especially if the choice is marrying an unbelieving partner whose life is completely out of compliance with the Scriptures. With God nothing is impossible, but there are some things that prayer will not change, if and when we decide to make decisions that are inconsistent with the will of God for our life.

The Bible gives us a vivid description of the life and ministry of King Saul, a leader known for his presumptuousness and disobedience, who made decisions that grieved the heart of God.

> Then the word of the Lord came to Samuel, saying, I regret making Saul king, for he has turned back from following Me and has not performed My commands. And Samuel was grieved and angry [with Saul], and he cried to the Lord all night.
>
> —1 Samuel 15:10–11

A leader can choose to disobey God and put his or her personal preference or agenda above the responsibility and requirements of his spiritual assignment. He or she can also choose to neglect the spiritual needs of the people entrusted to their care. This act of disobedience affects the minister, the ministry, and the people governed by the minister. There can be no elevation where there is disobedience.

Satan hates women. It was through a woman that the Redeemer came into the world; she is the birthing channel for habitation in the earth realm. Satan uses every weapon at his disposal to subject women to every kind of abuse, deception, defamation, exploitation, discrimination, and victimization. There are assignments placed on single women in positions of authority and leadership in ministry. Not only is she discriminated against by men, but she is disrespected by some women also. And there are men who purposely target ministries that are pastored by women with the intent to add it to their list of conquests...or to get their hands on the resources of the ministry. When women in ministry marry unsaved men, not only is it disobedience but it is also out of desperation because of the relentless warfare against women in ministry.

On the other hand, men who come to the house of God because of their wives can be good supporters and benefactors to the church; yet some never develop their own relationship with God. But those who do respond to the Spirit of God and begin to seek and pursue God can develop their own personal relationship with God.

We do not see in people what God sees unless we have the gift of discernment. Man looks on the outward appearance, but God looks in and on the heart. He searches the heart and knows the thoughts and the intent of man. It is out of the abundance of the heart that the mouth speaks, and God said that the heart is desperately wicked and deceitful above all things (Jer. 17:9), and only God can test and try the heart of man.

> The heart is deceitful above all things, and it is exceedingly perverse and corrupt and severely, mortally sick! Who can know it [perceive, understand, be acquainted with his own heart and mind]?
> —JEREMIAH 17:9

In this age, the women of this current generation in Western cultures are seeking and defining who they want for a husband. Any woman aspiring to be married, who is not just looking for a mediocre relationship with a man, should have some prerequisites outlining what she is looking for in a husband. All men take into consideration what he first sees with his eyes, and depending on his disposition, he may be looking for a woman with certain qualities, such as her physical attraction, her financial independence, her level of education, her skills and talents, and whether or not she is spiritually inclined and morally sound. When God brought the woman to the man in the Garden of Eden, the man did not need any of the above qualifications. What he needed was companionship because he had everything a mortal man needed to be dominant in the earth, except a companion. When God introduced the man to his wife, Adam said, "This [creature] is now bone of my bones and flesh of my flesh" (Gen. 2:23).

Gender or accomplishments does not define whether a man will be a good husband or a good father. Most men who were raised in single-parent households without a father have issues that a woman cannot resolve or understand. But Jesus Christ is inviting all men to walk the path to becoming fulfilled by being conformed to His image, as he is a man of God, a husband, and a father.

Women who are seeking and searching for a husband must be careful because women are more emotional than they are practical and often will fall in love with someone who is immature, unreliable, good looking, broke, and who is not looking for a long-term relationship.

A crafty woman will use her flesh, gifts, money, material things, and whatever is at her disposal to entice a man. But what she does not understand is this: whatever ploy she uses to entice a man who is not in love with her, she will have to continue using the same ploy to keep the man interested. Therefore, it is much better if a man falls in love with a woman and chooses the woman to be his lifelong companion. If a woman manipulates a man into marriage, she will have to use everything at her disposal to control the relationship and keep the man interested, and if the man is not compliant and is stubborn, the marriage will eventually end in divorce. No man wants to please a woman he is not in love with.

> He who finds a [true] wife finds a good thing and obtains favor from the Lord.
> —PROVERBS 18:22

> House and riches are the inheritance from fathers, but a wise, understanding, and prudent wife is from the Lord.
> —PROVERBS 19:14

A precious woman of God whom I love dearly met a man not too long after her divorce from her first husband. She divorced after years of abuse and months of separation, and then she was finally free, but she was lonely and desperate. Not too long after her divorce, she met a man who made his living driving a cab. He lived in a room somewhere and had nothing besides his clothes and his bed. He too was divorced from his first wife and maintained a go-nowhere, achieve-nothing existence until he met my friend, who fell in love, brought him to church, and introduced him to her children.

At first, he did not want to marry her, but she convinced the church that the Lord said this was her mate. The church prayed and prayed until he agreed and they got married. He moved out of his room to her posh home in the suburbs, and his life was good. He traded in his raggedy cab and bought a new vehicle. He took his place assisting her in the ministry and was ordained as an elder. But one day, he asked her to put her house in his name. He had already told his people that the house belonged to him. His wife responded by saying, "This house belongs to my children." He retaliated with rage and threats of divorce. He picked fights with her children and began to slander his wife's name in the community and among the church members. Finally he left the marriage and the church. His status in life changed, but his heart never changed.

Many women are married today because they pursued their husbands, bought their own ring, paid for the wedding, and provided the man with a dowry, which was her house and home. Even though some kept men may be working, the wife is the financier for the household. One woman told me, "My husband is slow; he did not know the will of God for his life, I had to tell him, God said, 'We have to be married,'" and he did marry her.

Another woman told me that she met her husband at work. They were good friends. He was going through a divorce and shared with her all the trials and tribulations he was having with his wife. She fell in love with him, but he was not in love with her. She was advised by another woman to tell him how she felt, and she did. She proposed to him, he accepted, and they got married.

Women who get their husbands by deception and by encroaching on another woman's territory are always suspicious and threatened when other women are friendly and responsive to their husbands. Their thought is always this: "I know how I got him, so another woman with assets can offer the same privileges. Since he is so vulnerable, he can always say yes to someone else."

In this generation, women are taking it upon themselves to point the man in the direction of marriage because some men see marriage as bondage. Many of them see the financial responsibility of maintaining a family and would rather live in a common-law arrangement so that they could make an escape without having to divorce and lose their vital assets. Other men cannot conceive the thought of being in a committed relationship with one woman. Some have had bad experiences with the wrong woman and are afraid of commitment.

Some are too immature for marriage. But with the breakdown of morals and family values in our society, our children and the church have lost something quite valuable—the precious gift of the family.

IDENTIFYING AREAS OF WEAKNESS IN SPIRITUAL COVERING

> Then Jonathan said, My father has troubled the land. See how my eyes have brightened because I tasted a little of this honey.
> —1 SAMUEL 14:29

According to my understanding, spiritual covering is very vital because it is supposed to provide protection, security, direction, a working relationship, and assistance with the work of the kingdom. But sometimes the covering we choose is too inadequate.

If you are a woman in ministry, your covering is an essential part of your spiritual armor. You must have a relationship with a covering that you can touch because communication is vital to the relationship and covenant. Because of Satan's warfare against women, her covering is a vital part of her protective shield.

The apostle Paul gave his spiritual son Timothy insight into the times and spiritual condition of the hearts of men at the end of this age. He said:

> But understand this, that in the last days will come [set in] perilous times of great stress and trouble [hard to deal with and hard to bear].
>
> For people will be lovers of self and [utterly] self-centered, lovers of money and aroused by an inordinate [greedy] desire for wealth, proud and arrogant and contemptuous boasters. They will be abusive (blasphemous, scoffing), disobedient to parents, ungrateful, unholy and profane.
>
> [They will be] without natural [human] affection (callous and inhuman), relentless (admitting of no truce or appeasement); [they will be] slanderers (false accusers, troublemakers), intemperate and loose in morals and conduct, uncontrolled and fierce, haters of good.
>
> [They will be] treacherous [betrayers], rash, [and] inflated with self-conceit. [They will be] lovers of sensual pleasures and vain amusements more than and rather than lovers of God.
>
> For [although] they hold a form of piety (true religion), they deny and reject and are strangers to the power of it [their conduct belies the

genuineness of their profession]. Avoid [all] such people [turn away from them].

For among them are those who worm their way into homes and captivate silly and weak-natured and spiritually dwarfed women, loaded down with [the burden of their] sins [and easily] swayed and led away by various evil desires and seductive impulses.

[These weak women will listen to anybody who will teach them]; they are forever inquiring and getting information, but are never able to arrive at a recognition and knowledge of the Truth.

Now just as Jannes and Jambres were hostile to and resisted Moses, so these men also are hostile to and oppose the Truth. They have depraved and distorted minds, and are reprobate and counterfeit and to be rejected as far as the faith is concerned.

—2 Timothy 3:1–8

Areas of weakness in spiritual covering are:

- Being a lover of self (self is priority, the worship of self)

- Being a lover of money (covetous, greedy)

- Lacking the love of God (egotistical, vain, without the heart of God)

- Preaching slander (gossip and lies) in the pulpit

- Pride, arrogance, being boastful, stubborn, lying

- Being ungrateful (unthankful)

- Immorality (uncontrolled sexual appetite)

- Being a lover of sensual pleasure (manipulative, flirtatious, addicted)

- Being pretentious (having a form of piety, godliness, and righteousness)

- Taking into captivity spiritually weak and immoral women

- Resisting truth and having no revelation (they use the commandments of men as their doctrine)

- Hating correction (loving flattery)

- Despising those who are good (jealousy)

- Breaking covenant

- Lacking order in the house of God

- Controlling and manipulating (spirit of Jezebel)

In the kingdom of God, there is governmental order, rank, responsibility, justice, judgment, mercy, and forgiveness. God is a God of order. He is not the author of confusion. In teaching His disciples how to pray, Jesus taught them to pray, "Thy kingdom come and thy will be done on earth as it is in heaven" (Matt. 6:10). It is the will of God that the same order, government, rank, and authority in heaven be manifested on Earth. "Thy kingdom come" speaks of the elements of the spiritual kingdom of God, which are righteousness, peace and joy in the Holy Ghost, which comes to reside in every born-again believer.

Many people have learned how to mask their pain and their dysfunction until a situation triggers a manifestation or God pulls the covers off and exposes them. Pastor George Beck was married to a woman whose spirit was out of order. She was the cause of many problems in the church. She kept the church divided and created problems for anyone serving in an official capacity.

This pastor's wife, whom we will refer to as Becky, became my first case study. Becky had a lot of issues that stemmed from abuse and neglect in her childhood. She lacked that nurturing love that parents give to children; therefore, Becky did not love herself and could not love anybody else. She suffered from rejection, low self-esteem, jealousy, and all the indiscretions that are associated with that type of dysfunction. She began having an affair with someone she admired, and her first two children were born out of that relationship.

Her affair was with a young Bible school student who was on his way to becoming a pastor. He had recently graduated from Bible college and was engaged to a wonderful Christian woman whom he had met at Bible college. After their marriage, they were in line to be appointed as pastors in a very prestigious organization, yet he was having a secret affair with Becky. After some time, Becky got pregnant with her first child, and when she told the church elders whom she was pregnant by, he was forced to step down from his position in the ministry.

At first he denied the affair, but after Becky got pregnant with their second child, he was advised to marry her for the sake of the children. After their marriage he resumed his ministry and eventually started a church. But secretly he was abusing Becky verbally and physically. He was enraged because he was forced to marry a woman he did not love. The abuse at home along with her childhood issues inflamed her dysfunctional behavior. She took her rage to the church and caused havoc in the house of God.

Everyone had rallied around the fallen, young minister, trying to save him and his ministry, but no one counseled Becky. Her issues were never addressed. She became the pastor's wife and brought into the church all her baggage from her childhood: abuse, rejection, low self-esteem, resentment, jealousy, anger, unforgiveness, vindictiveness, and sabotage, all of which were unveiled as she took control of the church in her capacity as the pastor's wife and the voice of authority over every other leader and auxiliary in the church.

Her dysfunction was at the root of all the confusion in the church. Becky drove the church to its knees in prayer. As Becky took control of the church, the man looked the other way, surrendering his badge of authority and giving her complete control. He had become weary with the relentless fighting, which was affecting his health, his finances, and the ministry.

But this was a praying church. However, the church would only experience spasmodic showers of revival and minimal growth despite all the evangelistic efforts that were done in the community. Even when there was growth, Becky sabotaged the work of that auxiliary. She stirred up discord, created strife, and brought confusion in the ranks. Eventually, all the young ministers took their families and left the church.

This started a prayer vigil for divine intervention. A shaking came to the church, and God began removing the pillars (key leaders in vital ministries). Each time a pillar was removed, the department affected fell into disarray and chaos. Eventually there was a split in the church, and most of the members abandoned the church, leaving four people behind: the pastor, his wife, and their two sons. They were eventually thrown out of the rented building, and the church was dissolved.

> Remember then from what heights you have fallen. Repent (change the inner man to meet God's will) and do the works you did previously [when first you knew the Lord], or else I will visit you and remove your lampstand from its place, unless you change your mind and repent.
>
> —Revelation 2:5

When the head is out of order, the body will be out of order. What sits on the head will flow down to the body. If there is chaos at the head, there will be chaos in the body. If there is dysfunction in the pastor's home, that spirit will invade and infest the church.

I was too young to understand the dynamics of the situation going on at church, but this was my first lesson in the discernment of spirits and the beginning of a lifelong ministry of prayer. I personally believe there should be a special ministry to pastors' wives. They need other women of similar calling and experience who can minister to them, especially if they are young and spiritually immature and their husbands are depending on them to share the burden of family and ministry.

In Becky's case, the elders and ministers were so intent on respecting her office as the pastor's wife that no one diagnosed or discerned her problems until it was too late. And those who did said nothing to her directly. They just talked among themselves. But this wounded woman was the doorway through which the seeds of discord were sown in the church, which eventually had devastating consequences in the lives of many people. Many of them left the church and walked away from God. They were so wounded, offended, and fed up with all the nonsense, and some of them never went back to any church and fell like seed by the wayside.

There is a wise saying that I must quote at this time: there is safety in numbers. I want to add to it: there is safety in covenant relationships. When a local church is under internal stress, this attracts the forces of darkness. The enemy could smell discord and dissention in the ranks like a shark could smell blood. They attack when churches are disconnected, weak, and vulnerable.

However, the wisdom I gained from this story is this: No local church should have to endure the attacks of the enemy alone. We should have covenant relationships and alliances with other men of God who can pray for the church, give godly advice, and impart their wisdom to the leadership. Anointed prayer by men of rank in the Spirit can create a hedge and a shield to adequately protect the flock and divert the offensive strategies of the enemy, thus enabling the church to correct the situation and bring order to the house of God.

That hedge was not in place in this instance because the pastor was not in covenant relationship with any other ministry leader or local church. When he was a young man, there were people in place to assist him when he fell, but after twenty-five years in ministry, those relationships were no longer there. In his arrogance and defiance, he refused to submit to the governing authority of the organization and would not receive advice, correction, or wise counsel. Eventually, not too long after the split, the church was completely abandoned and the candlestick removed.

In studying the life of King Saul, the first king of Israel, we will observe that apart from his anointing as king, Saul had certain character flaws that eventually caused his demise as king. When his seat of authority was established, he began to act independently of God and the prophet Samuel. It never entered into his thoughts at any time to bring up the ark of the covenant, which represented God's government, or even to seek after it. The ark was a fixture in the tabernacle of Moses, but it had been out of its place for many years, since the death of Eli and his two sons, Hophni and Phinehas.

Saul had a humble beginning but became self-centered, rebellious, and disobedient. He was an unwise, prideful man who was deliberately contrary to the instructions of God given to him by Samuel. He refused to submit to Samuel, who was the prophetic voice, who had the Word of the Lord for the king and for the nation. He made a feeble attempt to seek the Lord by building an altar, but God did not answer him, so he blamed his son Jonathan. Saul had a tendency to blame everyone else for his blunders.

> And Saul built an altar to the Lord; it was the first altar he built to the Lord.
>
> Then Saul said, Let us go down after the Philistines by night and seize and plunder them until daylight, and let us not leave a man of them. They said, Do whatever seems good to you. Then the priest said, Let us draw near here to God.
>
> And Saul asked counsel of God, Shall I go down after the Philistines? Will You deliver them into the hand of Israel? But He did not answer him that day.
>
> —1 SAMUEL 14:35–37

King Saul was a father in Israel, yet Saul could not see beyond himself, his needs, and his ambitions. He was not spiritually perceptive and could not see that God was establishing a natural kingdom in Israel, which was to be a prototype of the spiritual kingdom of God that would be established at the coming of Christ, the Messiah, and the establishment of the church, the Holy Nation of God, first the natural kingdom then the spiritual kingdom.

He was content with building his own house (a type of the local church) and leaving the throne (the pastorate) as an inheritance to Jonathan, his firstborn son. When we first read of Saul, he was chasing donkeys. That was a learned behavior he acquired while working for his father. Upon becoming king, Saul resorted to his old ways; he chased anointed, gifted men like David and other valiant, fighting men whom God placed around him in his capacity as king to assist him in establishing the kingdom.

> Saul also went home to Gibeah; and there went with him a band of valiant men whose hearts God had touched.
>
> —1 SAMUEL 10:26

God had transitioned Israel from the era of the judges to the era of the kingdom. Samuel had written the manner and the dimensions of the kingdom, which he received from God, in a book for Saul to use as a point of reference. But as Saul fought the battles of the Lord and conquered Israel's enemies, pride, stubbornness, and rebellion entered his heart, and he refused to take counsel and instructions from Samuel, or to carry out all the specifics of the assignment God gave him concerning the Amalekites.

Herein lies the hidden danger of success in ministry: the enemy can plant a seed in the heart of a leader that would make him or her think that they could continue being successful apart from God. Then they begin to use their own wits, devices, and schemes, sometimes doing what God says but doing it their way.

> Samuel told Saul, The Lord sent me to anoint you king over His people Israel. Now listen and heed the words of the Lord.
>
> Thus says the Lord of hosts, I have considered and will punish what Amalek did to Israel, how he set himself against him in the way when [Israel] came out of Egypt.
>
> Now go and smite Amalek and utterly destroy all they have; do not spare them, but kill both man and woman, infant and suckling, ox and sheep, camel and donkey....
>
> Saul smote the Amalekites from Havilah as far as Shur, which is east of Egypt.
>
> And he took Agag king of the Amalekites alive, though he utterly destroyed all the rest of the people with the sword.

Saul and the people spared Agag and the best of the sheep, oxen, fatlings, lambs, and all that was good, and would not utterly destroy them; but all that was undesirable or worthless they destroyed utterly.

Then the word of the Lord came to Samuel, saying, I regret making Saul king, for he has turned back from following Me and has not performed My commands. And Samuel was grieved and angry [with Saul], and he cried to the Lord all night.

—1 SAMUEL 15:1–3, 7–11

I am not sure if King Saul knew the covenant God made with Moses and the children of Israel concerning the Amalekites. On their journey through the wilderness, Israel was attacked by the Amalekites, who were the descendants of Esau.

Then came Amalek [descendants of Esau] and fought with Israel at Rephidim.

And Moses said to Joshua, Choose us out men and go out, fight with Amalek. Tomorrow I will stand on the top of the hill with the rod of God in my hand.

So Joshua did as Moses said and fought with Amalek; and Moses, Aaron, and Hur went up to the hilltop.

When Moses held up his hand, Israel prevailed; and when he lowered his hand, Amalek prevailed.

But Moses' hands were heavy and grew weary. So [the other men] took a stone and put it under him and he sat on it. Then Aaron and Hur held up his hands, one on one side and one on the other side; so his hands were steady until the going down of the sun.

And Joshua mowed down and disabled Amalek and his people with the sword.

And the Lord said to Moses, Write this for a memorial in the book and rehearse it in the ears of Joshua, that I will utterly blot out the remembrance of Amalek from under the heavens.

And Moses built an altar and called the name of it, The Lord is my Banner;

And he said, Because [theirs] is a hand against the throne of the Lord, the Lord will have war with Amalek from generation to generation.

—EXODUS 17:8–16

Many generations later, God remembered the promise He made to Moses and Israel concerning the Amalekites, and He sent King Saul on an assignment to fulfill His word. By his disobedience, Saul delayed the judgment of God from coming to pass in the season and time that God had ordained for Amalek to reap the rewards of their bold defiance against the throne of God, which is the highest seat of authority and government in the spiritual and natural world. When he told Moses to write this judgment against Amalek in a book and keep it as a memorial. God meant business.

> And Moses built an altar and called the name of it, The Lord is my Banner; and he said, Because [theirs] is a hand against the throne of the Lord, the Lord will have war with Amalek from generation to generation.
>
> —Exodus 17:15–16

Once more Jonathan's word continued to be heard across the nation: "My father has troubled the land" (1 Sam. 14:29).

There are some people who are recognized and responded to spiritually more than others. It is what the spirit world recognizes when they encounter a servant of God. When Saul was anointed king, the effects of it were felt in the realm of the spirit and spiritually in him.

> Then the Spirit of the Lord will come upon you mightily, and you will show yourself to be a prophet with them; and you will be turned into another man.
>
> And when [Saul] had turned his back to leave Samuel, God gave him another heart, and all these signs came to pass that day.
>
> —1 Samuel 10:6, 9

Not only does the natural world witness our conversions, inaugurations, ordinations, and baptisms, but the spirit world does also, and they recognize rank, authority, and responsibility, and they respond accordingly.

> Therefore then, since we are surrounded by so great a cloud of witnesses [who have borne testimony to the Truth], let us strip off and throw aside every encumbrance (unnecessary weight) and that sin which so readily (deftly and cleverly) clings to and entangles us, and

let us run with patient endurance and steady and active persistence
the appointed course of the race that is set before us.

—HEBREWS 12:1

Their witness carries more weight, for it is from them we derive our supernatural assistance or with whom we wrestle. But sloth, disobedience, infidelity, and pride are the catalysts that diminish the fire fueling our respective ministries. Persistent disobedience and other sins contaminate the garment of the child of God, who is dressed in the Spirit with fine, linen robes, clean and white.

> Then, addressing me, one of the elders [of the heavenly Sanhedrin] said, Who are these [people] clothed in the long white robes? And from where have they come?
>
> I replied, Sir, you know. And he said to me, These are they who have come out of the great tribulation (persecution), and have washed their robes and made them white in the blood of the Lamb.
>
> —REVELATION 7:13–14

> And to her was granted that she should be arrayed in fine linen, clean and white: for the fine linen is the righteousness of saints.
>
> —REVELATION 19:8, KJV

Unlike Adam, who lost his entire covering, which was the glory of God, disobedience, and all sins appear as stains, blemishes, spots, and wrinkles on our white robes, which can only be purged by the blood of Jesus. These are spots of darkness on the garments of light that the believer is clothed in. These stains darken the glow of the glory of God and alert the spirit world to the change in status of the servant of God.

Some years ago I was the spiritual covering for a young couple. One night the Lord showed them to me in a dream. They were in church standing with the membership, praising God. Everybody had on bright white robes, except these two. Their robes were discolored, and the discoloration showed up quite clearly next to the lily white, stainless robes of the others. I fell on my knees and began interceding for them before I called. This young couple was still attending church but were having knock-down drag-out fights with each other, and their verbal abuse of each other was not pleasing to God. The wife was contending for control, and her defiant husband would not have it. When I called and told them what the Lord showed me, they repented of their foolishness.

Demons react with much delight to the opportunity of getting a shot at a servant of God. They have instructions how they are to respond in such cases and are compelled by God to handle the servant of God the way God has determined. Angels must fade into the background until the matter between the believer and God is resolved, however long it takes.

Saul, like so many fathers, allowed ego, spiritual blindness, presumption, pride, greed, and infidelity to harden his heart, causing him to resist humility and repentance, therefore making an emphatic decision to walk contrary to God. I asked the Lord this question: "How do You discipline the sons of God who are standing behind pulpits who assume they are above correction?" The Lord said to me, "I take fruit away from them, and the church begins to lose members." People are the church's most vital asset. Without people, the ministry stagnates spiritually and suffers financially.

Several things can happen both in the natural and in the realm of the spirit when a servant of God is in a disobedient and in an unrepentant state:

- A change in helpers takes place in the spirit; angelic assistance recedes; sometimes they are reassigned because now the servant of God is in direct conflict with God.

- The candlestick is removed, the ministry falls to the ground, the light is extinguished, and the ministry dies.

- A new leader is anointed to replace the fallen leader, as in the case of King Saul and his successor David.

- King Saul's covering anointing was removed, and it was replaced by an evil spirit sanctioned by God.

Saul continued in office for about twenty years after his rejection by God, and after the anointing left him. He still sat on his throne and was still recognized as the king, but there was no communication between him and God.

Once again, Saul was turned into another man. His heart was now filled with murder, jealousy, and hate because he recognized that the anointing and mantle was now on David, and he was determined to do everything in his power, and with the authority of his office as king, to stop David from coming into his divine destiny. This became his obsession.

But the Spirit of the Lord departed from Saul, and an evil spirit from the Lord tormented and troubled him.

Saul's servants said to him, Behold, an evil spirit from God torments you.

—1 Samuel 16:14–15

When Adam lost the glory, he lost his anointing and covering. When the anointing lifts, the covering is removed and the godly seal is broken. It is replaced by lying spirits that perform similar signs and wonders, deceiving people into thinking nothing has changed.

For rebellion *is as* the sin of witchcraft, and stubbornness *is as* iniquity and idolatry. Because you have rejected the word of the Lord, He also has rejected you from *being* king.

—1 Samuel 15:23, nkjv

As we study the life of Saul after his rejection by God, what we see is a father's fall from grace and his attempts to kill David, the man chosen by God to replace him. Samuel, his spiritual adviser, died. The Philistines, who were Israel's nemesis, continued to wage war against Israel relentlessly, partly because of Saul's disobedience and because the nation had also disobeyed God and turned to idolatry.

Toward the end of his life, Saul plunged into the depths of despair and degradation and sought help from a witch. That action sealed his fate. He, along with three of his sons, died in battle the next day. It was an Amalekite, the enemy of God whom Saul refused to slaughter, who brought the news to David that Saul and his sons were dead, and he took credit for his death. (See 1 Samuel 28, 31; 2 Samuel 1.)

Jonathan knew of his father's spiritual and mental depredation. He knew the Lord had departed from his father. Yet Jonathan continued to associate himself and to play an important role in his father's fallen ministry, which was now under the control of an evil spirit. Jonathan did the right thing by being in covenant with David, God's chosen man of the hour. It was through David that Jonathan and his seed would be blessed. But Jonathan remained committed to fight alongside his father in battle even though he knew he could not save him, and they died together at the hands of the Philistines.

Jonathan is like so many spiritual sons of fallen fathers who never separate themselves even after the anointing departs, and God is no longer present.

These sons stick around for what they think they are entitled to because of the years they invested in their father's ministry, but God can replace whatever was lost or stolen if our investment was in the kingdom and not in a man.

HEADSHIP, THE POWER OF AGREEMENT, AND THE LOCAL CHURCH

Behold, how good and how pleasant it is. For brethren to dwell together in unity! It is like the precious oil upon the head, running down on the beard, the beard of Aaron, running down on the edge of his garments.

—PSALM 133:1–2

Headship denotes governmental authority. The responsibility of headship is not to dominate, control, disrespect, use, or abuse others, but to teach, direct, correct, instruct, discipline, encourage, identify, validate, and promote.

But Jesus called them to *Himself* and said, "You know that the rulers of the Gentiles lord it over them, and those who are great exercise authority over them.

Yet it shall not be so among you; but whoever desires to become great among you, let him be your servant.

And whoever desires to be first among you, let him be your slave—just as the Son of Man did not come to be served, but to serve, and to give His life a ransom for many.

—MATTHEW 20:25–28

Respect is defined as:[6]

- To feel or show honor or esteem for someone

- To hold in high regard

- To consider or treat with deference or dutiful regard

- To show consideration for

- To avoid intruding upon or interfering with others

- Courteous expressions of honor

> Let the elders who rule well be counted worthy of double honor, especially those who labor in the word and doctrine.
>
> —1 TIMOTHY 5:17

Leaders should know "the fear of God." The fear of God causes leaders to reverence the office they hold. First, there must be reverence for God and then respect for oneself and respect for the people.

The church is a holy nation, and all nations have some form of government. The governmental leaders in the house of God have spiritual authority. When spiritual authority is violated and a headship gift is disrespected, it is a violation and an attack against the throne of God, which is the highest seat of spiritual authority in the universe. It is from His throne God dispenses justice and judgment as He presides over His house and intervenes in the affairs of men.

The government of the church is carried upon the shoulders of Jesus Christ, who is the head of the church and the Savior of the body of believers. The authority exercised by designated leaders can only come from Jesus Christ. We are not to fear leadership, but we must honor leadership. Leaders are assigned by God to watch for our souls; therefore, they are accountable to God for the souls entrusted to their spiritual care. Leaders must not only preach and teach the Word of God, but they must also lead and teach by being moral and spiritual examples.

> Obey them that have the rule over you, and submit yourselves: for they watch for your souls, as they that must give account, that they may do it with joy, and not with grief: for that is unprofitable for you.
>
> —HEBREWS 13:17, KJV

These anointed headship gifts or rulers over the house of God are persons who are called and chosen by God and have been given a great responsibility to watch and care for the souls that make up the household of faith. This is a responsibility that no man should take lightly, an honor that no man should take upon himself, because those whom God has sent, He takes an account of their works and services and rewards us accordingly.

> And the Lord said, Who then is that faithful steward, the wise man whom his master will set over those in his household service to supply them their allowance of food at the appointed time?
>
> Blessed (happy and to be envied) is that servant whom his master finds so doing when he arrives.

Truly I tell you, he will set him in charge over all his possessions.

But if that servant says in his heart, My master is late in coming, and begins to strike the menservants and the maids and to eat and drink and get drunk,

The master of that servant will come on a day when he does not expect him and at an hour of which he does not know, and will punish him and cut him off and assign his lot with the unfaithful.

And that servant who knew his master's will but did not get ready or act as he would wish him to act shall be beaten with many [lashes].

But he who did not know and did things worthy of a beating shall be beaten with few [lashes]. For everyone to whom much is given, of him shall much be required; and of him to whom men entrust much, they will require and demand all the more.

—Luke 12:42–48

Even though many churches have been raised up by God to minister to the family, the success of family life among the brethren also depends on the example set by spiritual fathers. There are many spiritual fathers in the body of Christ, as there are many natural fathers in society who never had a good relationship with their own father.

Men who have not been fathered lead by trial and error unless they are taught by the Holy Spirit and infused with the wisdom of God. The pattern of all things God created is in heaven. Fatherhood comes from God; He is the Father of all and the perfect example of fatherly characteristics and attributes. To prove His love for mankind, God manifested Himself through His Son, Jesus. Jesus is the sole expression of the glory of God, the perfect imprint and very image of His Father. (See Hebrews 1.)

Philip said to Him, Lord, show us the Father [cause us to see the Father--that is all we ask]; then we shall be satisfied.

Jesus replied, Have I been with all of you for so long a time, and do you not recognize and know Me yet, Philip? Anyone who has seen Me has seen the Father. How can you say then, Show us the Father?

Do you not believe that I am in the Father, and that the Father is in Me? What I am telling you I do not say on My own authority and of My own accord; but the Father Who lives continually in Me does the (His) works (His own miracles, deeds of power).

> Believe Me that I am in the Father and the Father in Me; or else
> believe Me for the sake of the [very] works themselves. [If you cannot
> trust Me, at least let these works that I do in My Father's name
> convince you.]
>
> —JOHN 14:8–11

The local church is the household of the God the Father. God is family oriented, and the family as God designed it is under constant attack by the powers of darkness, who arbitrarily want to redesign God's original plan and purpose for the family. Churches that minister to the family must take up the charge to intercede for the family of man and the generations that are to follow, because the blessings of God are generational. Believers who are family oriented must find a church that promulgates in its dogma—marriage between a man and a woman and the family as God ordained it—giving honor with love and without prejudice or preferential treatment to the male or the female.

If the power of agreement is in force between the man and his wife, the anointing on the head filters down to the family. If there is friction and dissension at the head, that spirit will affect the rest of the body. It is sad to say, but it is so true—men who had abusive fathers are also abusive to their wives. They are demanding and intimidating in their own homes, but the root of their behavior is the dysfunctional relationship the man had with his own father.

But when the male works in conjunction with the Word, the Spirit, and the Blood, and creates an environment in the home where prayers can be answered, angels can congregate, the anointing can flow, miracles can manifest, and Jesus Christ can be glorified, it establishes the Edenic order in the family, which is the order of God in the household of God.

> In the same way you married men should live considerately with
> [your wives], with an intelligent recognition [of the marriage relation],
> honoring the woman as [physically] the weaker, but [realizing that
> you] are joint heirs of the grace (God's unmerited favor) of life, in
> order that your prayers may not be hindered and cut off. [Otherwise
> you cannot pray effectively.]
>
> —1 PETER 3:7

The atmosphere and spiritual climate in the Garden of Eden, where God placed the man and his wife, is symbolic of the kingdom of God, which is within us: righteousness, peace, and joy in the Holy Ghost. Satan is a master manipulator of atmosphere. He can change the atmosphere in a home, a church, or a community by releasing spirits that will cause people to be hostile to one another, and he can create an environment where strife prevails.

After man fell, the garden was ultimately destroyed. But in God's plan of redemption, He relocated the kingdom of Eden. It is no longer a geographical location in the earth but a spiritual location within the earthen temple of man. Jesus said, to Nicodemus, "Except a man is born again, he cannot see the kingdom of God...Except a man be born of water and of the Spirit he cannot enter the kingdom of God" (John 3:3, 5). The kingdom of God is a treasure God has placed within the reborn spirit of man. "We possess this precious treasure [the divine Light of the Gospel] in [frail, human] vessels of earth, that the grandeur and exceeding greatness of the power may be shown to be from God and not from ourselves" (2 Cor. 4:7). The children of God are citizens of the kingdom of God and also members of the household of faith.

The local church is a natural and spiritual entity. In my book *While Men Slept*, there is a heading that states, "The House That God Did Not Build." It is a revelation that God gave to me about what goes on in the realm of the spirit with a church when the pastor (male) is not married.

God showed me through this vision how Satan built in the realm of the spirit another house that was attached to this specific local church, called the "House of Women." In that house Satan had certain women in captivity. All of the women in the vision were members of that local church. The house that Satan built was a harem of women who were the spirit wives or concubines of that unmarried pastor.

Before Jesus built His church, Jesus said, "The foxes have holes, the birds of the air have nests but the son of man has no where to lay his head" (Luke 9:58). Jesus is the head of the church, and He is the Savior of the body. Where does He rest His head? He rests His head on the body. The church is the body of Christ. Before He organized His church, He had nowhere to rest His head. The head denotes rulership and authority. As head of the church, Jesus can transmit His thoughts, His ideas, His mind, and His anointing to His body through governmental leadership, the government that rests on His shoulders.

First comes the natural. The natural is always indicative of a spiritual truth. "The two shall become one flesh" (Gen. 2:24) describes the union of the man and his wife in holy matrimony. A man cannot be the head of a woman that is not his wife; he can only be the head of a woman who he is in covenant with him. To be a husband, a man must have a wife. To be a father, a man must have children. These are two separate and distinctive roles. His wife is not his child, and his daughter is not his wife.

The apostle Paul said, "A man must love his wife as his own body, for he that loves his wife loves himself" (Eph. 5:28).

Jesus had to adhere to the same principles of law that God gave to Israel concerning marriage. He also had to fulfill the biblical mandate that God instituted in Eden for marriage. The first Adam was made a living soul. Jesus, the last Adam, was made living Spirit. Every seed has to produce after its kind. The seed or offspring Jesus raised up unto His brother Adam was a generation of sons, born again of the Spirit of God and the seed of the Word of God.

> That which is born of the flesh is flesh; and that which is born of the Spirit is spirit.
>
> —JOHN 3:6, KJV

Jesus is betrothed to His church. The church is comprised of all believers who are born of the Spirit. The church is not a denomination or a religion. It is a generation of born-again believers who are the sons of God and joint heirs with Jesus Christ.

A pastor who is not married should not counsel a woman without a witness present. A female pastor should have her husband or someone else present if she is counseling a man. Out of the mouth of two or three witnesses shall every word be established. This is proper protocol because it protects the pastor from the spirit of propaganda.

What is the common denominator in every environment? In the corporate environment, private enterprise, government agencies, other religious denominations, and the church, the common denominator is people. Without people, everything would be affected and some things would cease to exist. The gathering together of people with a common agenda presents an opportunity to share an ideology, to have dialogue, creativity, relationships, or networking for business enterprise. People are also very important to God; Jesus died for people. The church is comprised of people from every background, race, culture, language, financial status, ethnicity, and skin color.

THE NEED FOR DISCRETION

In the local church environment, personal and confidential information is always shared with leaders other than the pastor, as believers seek wise counsel and prayer. However, some leaders lack wisdom, and some people talk too much. There are pastors that have an open policy in their home and in the church; they talk about everything that is happening in the church with and around family members, even around underage children. It is unfortunate when people's personal business becomes a part of the sermon. However, there are too many people seeking godly counsel and prayer outside of their local church for fear that their personal information will find its way onto the church's propaganda bulletin board.

Negative information about church members and leaders has a tremendous impact on children because their hearts are tender. It also makes it difficult for an unsaved child or spouse to take the message of God's love by the church seriously. This lack of discretion with people's personal and private information has caused many people to be hurt by the church, the repercussions of which can be seen and felt as people leave the local church and begin to wander from church to church becoming unstable in their walk with God.

If they have no root or foundation in the Word, their relationship with God is affected. We have to grow where we have been planted by God. To be uprooted and planted in another environment in many instances is not beneficial for a young believer who has left the household of faith because of the indiscretions of a few believers. At every stage of development, there must be information that will nurture us and cause us to grow up into the stature of Jesus Christ, and every season in our growth and maturity is measured by our faithfulness in relation to our walk with the Lord.

The Lord also places us in an environment where our gifts can be pruned and enhanced and where we can be prepared to fulfill the call of God on our life. If you are a person blessed with gifts of the Spirit, a house whose basic Bible belief, discipline, and practice does not embrace the baptism of the Holy Spirit and the gifts of the Spirit is not the environment for one to mature in their walk with God, because their gifts can never be activated, embraced, or used in that environment.

Chapter 4

THE SPIRIT OF HARLOTRY

One of the seven angels who had the seven bowls then came and spoke to me, saying, Come with me! I will show you the doom (sentence, judgment) of the great harlot (idolatress) who is seated on many waters, [she] with whom the rulers of the earth have joined in prostitution (idolatry) and with the wine of whose immorality (idolatry) the inhabitants of the earth have become intoxicated.

And [the angel] bore me away [rapt] in the Spirit into a desert (wilderness), and I saw a woman seated on a scarlet beast that was all covered with blasphemous titles (names), and he had seven heads and ten horns.

The woman was robed in purple and scarlet and bedecked with gold, precious stones, and pearls, [and she was] holding in her hand a golden cup full of the accursed offenses and the filth of her lewdness and vice.

And on her forehead there was inscribed a name of mystery [with a secret symbolic meaning]: Babylon the great, the mother of prostitutes (idolatresses) and of the filth and atrocities and abominations of the earth.

I also saw that the woman was drunk, [drunk] with the blood of the saints (God's people) and the blood of the martyrs [who witnessed] for Jesus. And when I saw her, I was utterly amazed and wondered greatly.

—REVELATION 17:1–6

THE BEAST THAT CARRIED THE WOMAN WAS SYMBOLIC OF THE ROMAN empire. The city of Rome was the seat of operations for the beast (political Babylon). Mystery Babylon is the apostate ecclesiastical system that arose after the apostolic church that Jesus built went into apostasy.

The Jerusalem Bible translates Revelation 17:5: "On her forehead was written a name, cryptic name, indicating that 'Babylon' is meant symbolically."

The reason her name is written on the forehead is probably to identify her with the harlots of Rome. It was customary in Rome during the first century for the prostitutes to display their names on their foreheads. The mystery of this religious fornicator is hidden from the natural eyes and understanding of man. However, God has given to the sons of God understanding of the mysteries of the kingdom and the manifold wisdom of God. The term mystery also refers to her preoccupation with magic and sorcery, as Babylon of old. If she is the successor to the Old Testament Babylon, indications are that she is filled with mystical fascinations. A thorough study of the city of Babylon and the Babylonian Empire as it flourished in later years, especially under King Nebuchadnezzar will give further insight into the revelation of "Mystery Babylon."

Babylon had a very complex religious system that was refined, orderly, sophisticated, and controlled by a large priesthood serving in different temples throughout the city. Their chief god was Bel, "the lord," who they believed constantly sought to do mankind good. Their other gods were the sun, moon and stars, pagan deities, and idols. Their priests were sorcerers, magicians, and astrologers whose array of ritualistic worship was fascinating and extremely believable to the heathen world at that time. Babylon, therefore, has been symbolically used to denote the confused or drunken condition of the ecclesiastical system of the church in the last days.

Any institution or enterprise that God ordains and sets in order, Satan will have a counterfeit. God has a body of believers; Satan has a body of unbelievers. Jesus has a bride; Satan has a bride. Jesus has a kingdom; Satan has a kingdom. Jesus has a kingdom message; Satan has a kingdom message. God has children; Satan has children. God has a plan of reconciliation, salvation, and restoration for mankind; Satan has a plan of death, murder, and destruction for mankind. These two kingdoms are directly opposed to one another in purpose, planning, concept, and design. God is truth, and Satan is the father of lies.

This spirit entity described in Revelation is the mother of harlots. *Mother* means one that has given birth. The true nature of harlotry is idolatry. Idolatry is the worship of idols, false religion, and false gods. The mother of harlots is the principality that is responsible for all false religion and their equivalent, including all forms of sexual perversion, such as incest, pedophilia, sodomy, prostitution, adultery, and fornication. She is also behind the drug culture.

The war on drugs is not only natural but also a spiritual war. The end results of those who have been captured in this warfare are always premature death, but the bondage is spiritual.

Idolatry is spiritual adultery. God called Israel a harlot because of her love affair with idols. As Israel made alliances with other nations, she adopted their form of ritualistic worship of demonic principalities such as Baal, Ashtoreth, and the queen of heaven. She despised her (marriage) covenant with Jehovah, yet none of the other nations chose to worshiped her God. Jehovah rebuked Israel through the prophets continually, yet she did not change her idolatrous ways.

> You have built also for yourself a vaulted chamber (brothel) and have made a high place [of idol worship] in every street.
>
> At every crossway you built your high place [for idol worship] and have made your beauty an abomination [abhorrent, loathsome, extremely disgusting, and detestable]; and you have made your body available to every passerby and multiplied your [idolatry and spiritual] harlotry.
>
> You have also played the harlot with the Egyptians, your neighbors, [by adopting their idolatries] whose worship is thoroughly sensuous, and you have multiplied your harlotry to provoke Me to anger.
>
> Behold therefore, I have stretched out My hand against you, diminished your ordinary allowance of food, and delivered you over to the will of those who hate and despise you, the daughters of the Philistines, who turned away in shame from your despicable policy and lewd behavior [for they are faithful to their gods]!
>
> You played the harlot also with the Assyrians because you were unsatiable; yes, you played the harlot with them, and yet you were not satisfied.
>
> Moreover, you multiplied your harlotry with the land of trade, with Chaldea, and yet even with this you were not satisfied.
>
> How weak and spent with longing and lust is your heart and mind, says the Lord God, seeing you do all these things, the work of a bold, domineering harlot.
>
> —Ezekiel 16:24–30

The spirit of harlotry is depicted as a woman in the spirit. The church is also depicted as a woman in the spirit. The harlot is the bride of Satan, and the church is the bride of Christ.

These two women have husbands who are fathers, and the seed of these two fathers are two lineages of children (people) in the earth: the children of God and the children of the devil. It does not matter what people group a person originates from, their skin color, culture, level of education, status in life, rich or poor, young or old, their religious persuasion, or language. Individually and spiritually we fall into one of these two categories of people.

> By this it is made clear who take their nature from God and are His children and who take their nature from the devil and are his children: no one who does not practice righteousness [who does not conform to God's will in purpose, thought, and action] is of God; neither is anyone who does not love his brother.
>
> —1 John 3:10

As God calls His sons into ministry, Satan also calls his sons into ministry. His "ministers" are known in different geographical locations as shamans, voodoo priests, witches, warlocks, witch doctors, physics, sorcerers, obeah men and women, necromancers, magicians, drug dealers, murderers, and spiritual hit men. All ministers of darkness are agents for bondage, destruction, and death, and they all fall under the ministry of the mother of harlots.

Now we will attempt to define the works, weapons, and warfare of the spirit of harlotry to expose her intent and purpose. One of the manifestations of the mother of harlots in the natural is adultery. There is spiritual adultery, and there is physical adultery. Her children are called *strange* children. Her warfare is to destroy the righteous seed of God, the home, the family, and the institution of marriage as it was designed by God. She fosters and facilitates the enmity between the seed of the woman and the seed of Satan. In her warfare against the plan and purpose of God for the holy estate of marriage, she uses many schemes based on the selfish, fallen nature of man, his indifference toward the precepts and commandments of God, the hardness of his heart, his lust for the flesh, the lust of the eye, and the pride of life.

The mother of harlots uses many weapons to ensnare and enflame the appetite of the male because of his vulnerability to the weakness of his flesh. Her weapon of choice is *flattery*.

> But every man is tempted, when he is drawn away of his own lust, and enticed. Then when lust hath conceived, it bringeth forth sin: and sin, when it is finished, bringeth forth death.
>
> —James 1:14–15

The law of yielding and bondage states:

> Do you not know that if you continually surrender yourselves to anyone to do his will, you are the slaves of him whom you obey, whether that be to sin, which leads to death, or to obedience which leads to righteousness (right doing and right standing with God)?
>
> —ROMANS 6:16

The spirit of harlotry is symbolized as a woman who is a mother. Eve, the first woman, wife of Adam, was "the mother of all the living." The church is also symbolized in the spirit realm as a mother. She is called the bride of Christ. God said to Satan, "The seed of the woman shall bruise your head" (Gen. 3:15). "Seed" refers to children birthed by the woman. Mothers have a peculiar assignment not only to nurture her seed but also to do warfare for her seed.

The spirit of harlotry blinds the man with flattery, flirtation, flesh, money, and power. When a man is overcome by the wiles of the strange woman and that spirit attaches itself to him, his deliverance can only come through the intercessory warfare of his wife.

> Let not your heart incline toward her ways, do not stray into her paths. For she has cast down many wounded; indeed, all her slain are a mighty host. Her house is the way to Sheol (Hades, the place of the dead), going down to the chambers of death.
>
> —PROVERBS 7:25–27

Morally and spiritually, a man's wife is in the position to protect the man from losing his assets to the spirit of harlotry. One of her roles as a wife is to intercede for her husband, but when a husband demoralizes and abuses his wife, he limits her ability to intercede for him against the spirit of harlotry; his action against her suspends the power of agreement.

When this demonic entity captures a man, its first retaliatory action is to systematically turn the man's heart against his wife so that he will see her as his nemesis. Then that spirit causes him to begin his verbal, emotional, mental, or physical assault on his wife, which is designed to incapacitate her, to damage her soul (the mind, will, emotions, and intellect), which is the seat of a personality.

Women who suffer from low self-esteem, have a distorted image of themselves, and if they marry men of substance they will identify with their husband's image—his prestige, fame, power, money, and business acumen so people can have the same perception of them. If their husband is flirtatious and prone to have relationships with other women outside of the marriage, these women would often be angry with the other woman because without the man, she has no identity or power. She lives in an environment and a world that was created by the man for his comfort and enjoyment, and he may not esteem her as highly or as valuable as he esteems himself and his comforts. Her worth to him is her physical assets, which are fleeting, and according to the nature of the beast, she knows that she can be replaced by another woman at any season in this man's life.

If he is verbally and physically abusive, her lack of self-confidence will perpetuate his assaults on her because she is emotionally or financially dependent on him. Too much emotion is an indication of how deeply hurt a woman is and how she has been traumatized by her warfare. Emotion leaves the woman drained, bewildered, sorrowful, hurt, wounded, very sensitive, depleted, confused, and bitter. If she does not forgive, release the problem, and seek inner healing, she will be governed by her emotions. Unhealed woman become very vindictive, suspicious, manipulative, and jealous of other women in happy relationships. Some hide their hurts behind a wall of pride and hard work, while others take on a victim's mentality, believing all men are cruel.

The nature of this warfare is spiritual, and the weapons used in this battle are spiritual weapons. Strategy and wisdom can only come from God. Women of God cannot use the same weapons that the strange woman uses. The strategy of the mother of harlots is to disarm her opposition (the wife) because an emotionally wounded wife is weak and cannot do strategic level warfare with wisdom and precision when she is controlled by her emotions. If she does, her warfare would be based on her anxieties and fears.

For this reason, women (wives) in the body of Christ need the support of each other with prayer, fellowship, and encouragement if this spirit strikes at home. They should be vigilant, not suspicious, for when this spirit is on the prowl, it can manifest as another woman or another man. Many women are realizing that it is not the other woman that is the problem in the marriage, sometimes it is the other man, and when the man of God (her husband) is not watching and praying, the wife has to be more vigilant and sober-minded, not just suspicious, complaining, and controlling.

[Discretion shall watch over you, understanding shall keep you] to deliver you from the alien woman, from the outsider with her flattering words, who forsakes the husband and guide of her youth and forgets the covenant of her God.

For her house sinks down to death and her paths to the spirits [of the dead]. None who go to her return again, neither do they attain or regain the paths of life.

—PROVERBS 2:16–19

The assignment against headship (husbands) is to distract and disable the man, to cause him to lose focus and direction spiritually, mentally, and financially; to alienate him from his seed so that he will abandon his responsibilities to his children. Ultimately, Satan's plan is to capture the man's seed.

The spirit of harlotry uses the natural sexual appetite of the man to keep him under her control. The temptation to have sexual affairs outside of marriage is an ever-present evil. Her strategy is for the man to father children outside the covenant relationship of marriage, which will obligate the man financially to a relationship with a strange woman for years. In 90 percent of cases where a man has fathered a child outside of the home, his marriage ends in divorce. When the other woman bears seed for a married man, this is an insult levied at the wife. In the realm of the spirit, the other woman becomes his concubine or spirit wife. The Bible warns us to flee fornication because sex outside of marriage triggers bondage to the spirit of harlotry.

For by means of a whorish woman a man is brought to a piece of bread: and the adultress will hunt for the precious life.
—PROVERBS 6:26, KJV

But whoever commits adultery with a woman lacks heart and understanding (moral principle and prudence); he who does it is destroying his own life.
—PROVERBS 6:32

If the wife came from a home where she was never validated by her father and she lacked that nurturing love that parents give to children in their formative years, she may not know who she is internally, or she may not know what her strengths and weaknesses are, or what kind of armory she has to work with. Fathers give to daughters their identity and their strength, but there are some strong women who have never been validated by a father, yet they have found their identity and have gained strength and victory through life's adversity and their trust in God.

HARLOTRY AND THE SPIRIT OF CONFUSION

> When the human race began to increase, with more and more daughters being born, the sons of God noticed that the daughters of men were beautiful. They looked them over and picked out wives for themselves.
>
> This was back in the days (and also later) when there were giants in the land. The giants came from the union of the sons of God and the daughters of men.
> —GENESIS 6:1–2; 4–6, THE MESSAGE BIBLE

God has other methods of communication besides the spoken and written word. Dreams and visions are another form of revelation; they are part of a big picture that God will reveal to us frame by frame.

Whenever I have a dream or vision of an animal as the main character, it is an alert that an unclean spirit is about to manifest, or it is God's way of telling me that the root cause of the present problem I am experiencing is interference from an unclean spirit. A snake is symbolic of a deadly enemy. A dog is symbolic of a spirit of confusion.

There are people who were conceived through the union of a parent with a spirit of confusion, and they are the source of contention and strife in any environment. They are always involved in conflicts, backbiting, disagreements, misunderstandings, verbal assaults, and physical combat with their peers.

There is a young lady who I will call Dinah who was new to our congregation. As I was also new to that congregation we became friendly, but as time went by I realized that Dinah was a very talkative, competitive, and a loud person who would do anything to get attention. She came from a large family, but each child had a different biological father, and the mother was married to a man who was not the father of any of her children. This brood of children fought each other all the time; then they would join forces with each other to fight their neighbors. Dinah brought this spirit of confusion, lack of order, and disrespect for authority into the congregation.

One night, I had a vision of Dinah and I walking down the street. She was doing all the talking while I was just listening. During the conversation I turned my head and saw a big dog following us. I continued listening to her while keeping an eye on this dog. After a while the vision lifted, and I got up and began to pray in the Spirit. The Holy Spirit revealed to me that the dog in the vision was a spirit of confusion.

If God is not the author of confusion, then where does confusion originate? As I began to seek for understanding about the nature and assignment of the spirit of confusion, I realized that God created everything for a distinct purpose and function. There is order in His design and creation, and there are laws that govern and uphold everything that He has put in place. When people try to reinvent or recreate God's original design, it causes confusion if it is not according to the order of God. (For example, a man trying to impregnate another man is out of order with God's creation. Men are not created with the equipment to give birth to children.)

A spirit of confusion can come into manifestation in the life of people who are operating outside of the order of God. It manifests in their life, their business, their marriage, their relationships, and in any environment that they are a part of.

Here are some facts that will determine whether a spirit of confusion is present:

- If a person's birth father and mother are first-generation blood relatives, a spirit of confusion is present.

- If a daughter is impregnated by her natural father, a spirit of confusion is present.

- If a woman is pregnant by her sister's husband, a spirit of confusion is present.

- If a mother and her daughter are having sexual relationship with the same man, a spirit of confusion is present.

- If a brother and sister are having sexual relations, a spirit of confusion is present.

- If living or deceased parents had any involvement in the occult, a spirit of confusion is in the bloodline.

- When the spirit of incest is prevalent in a family, a spirit of confusion is present.

- If a brood of children have the same mother but each child was fathered by a different man, a spirit of confusion is present.

- If a person enters a blood covenant with the occult, a spirit of confusion is present.

- If a person practices different kinds of religion, a spirit of confusion is present.

- If a person has sex with animals, a spirit of confusion is present.

- When a person has multiple sex partners, a spirit of confusion is present.

The Bible warns against the spirit of confusion in the bloodline in the following text:

> None of you shall approach to any that is near of kin to him, to uncover their nakedness: I am the LORD.
>
> The nakedness of thy father, or the nakedness of thy mother, shalt thou not uncover: she is thy mother; thou shalt not uncover her nakedness.
>
> The nakedness of thy father's wife shalt thou not uncover: it is thy father's nakedness.
>
> The nakedness of thy sister, the daughter of thy father, or daughter of thy mother, whether she be born at home, or born abroad, even their nakedness thou shalt not uncover.
>
> The nakedness of thy son's daughter, or of thy daughter's daughter, even their nakedness thou shalt not uncover: for theirs is thine own nakedness.
>
> The nakedness of thy father's wife's daughter, begotten of thy father, she is thy sister, thou shalt not uncover her nakedness.
>
> Thou shalt not uncover the nakedness of thy father's sister: she is thy father's near kinswoman.
>
> Thou shalt not uncover the nakedness of thy mother's sister: for she is thy mother's near kinswoman.
>
> Thou shalt not uncover the nakedness of thy father's brother, thou shalt not approach to his wife: she is thine aunt.
>
> Thou shalt not uncover the nakedness of thy daughter in law: she is thy son's wife; thou shalt not uncover her nakedness.

Thou shalt not uncover the nakedness of thy brother's wife: it is thy brother's nakedness.

Thou shalt not uncover the nakedness of a woman and her daughter, neither shalt thou take her son's daughter, or her daughter's daughter, to uncover her nakedness; for they are her near kinswomen: it is wickedness.

Neither shalt thou take a wife to her sister, to vex her, to uncover her nakedness, beside the other in her life time.

Also thou shalt not approach unto a woman to uncover her nakedness, as long as she is put apart for her uncleanness.

Moreover thou shalt not lie carnally with thy neighbour's wife, to defile thyself with her.

—LEVITICUS 18:6–20, KJV

How does one get delivered from a spirit of confusion? The Bible tells us the story of a young man who was more honorable than all his brethren, but because his mother gave birth to him with sorrow, she named him Jabez. His name meant "he who causes sorrow," or "the sorrow maker." That name was an indictment against him. His mother put a stigma on Jabez because of her painful experience in giving birth to him. But when he grew up, he took his case to God and petitioned God to remove the stigma attached to him because of the name his mother gave him and the implications of that name.

Jabez was honorable above his brothers; but his mother named him Jabez [sorrow maker], saying, Because I bore him in pain.

Jabez cried to the God of Israel, saying, Oh, that You would bless me and enlarge my border, and that Your hand might be with me, and You would keep me from evil so it might not hurt me! And God granted his request.

—1 CHRONICLES 4:9–10

Single women and single men can make up a large percentage of the membership of a local church; therefore, the church is another environment where the spirit of harlotry may operate. The Bible states that the wheat and the tares must grow together until the time of harvest. This spirit prowls the hallways of churches, looking for opportunity. Even though it is depicted as a woman in the spirit, this spirit is genderless in the natural. It operates in the male as well as the female. If a pastor is captured by the spirit of harlotry, his ministry will suffer because he has opened the door and has given access to it, and it will invade his household as well as the house of God.

Ministers of God are supposed to maintain a standard of holiness and righteousness before God and before the people. If a minister is captured by the mother of harlots, he or she should pray and seek for help from other ministers before their reputation is tarnished and their ministry is affected.

THE STRANGE WOMAN; THE LOOSE WOMAN

For the commandment is a lamp, and the whole teaching [of the law] is light, and reproofs of discipline are the way of life, to keep you from the evil woman, from the flattery of the tongue of a loose woman.
—PROVERBS 6:23–24

Say unto wisdom, Thou art my sister; and call understanding thy kinswoman: that they may keep thee from the strange woman, from the stranger which flattereth with her words.
—PROVERBS 7:4–5, KJV

In her capacity as a mother, the spirit of harlotry has given birth to strange and loose women. She has children on assignment in the earth. All it takes for one to align himself with a spirit entity is a decision. Israel made a decision to worship idols, and she became a nation of harlots or adulterers. When a man or woman makes a decision and comes into agreement with the doctrine or philosophy of devils, they can be a channel or doorway of entry for that spirit to promote its activities and philosophies in the earth.

HER SEDUCTION, WARFARE,
AND WEAPONS OF WAR

But every man is tempted, when he is drawn away of his own lust, and enticed. Then when lust hath conceived, it bringeth forth sin: and sin, when it is finished, bringeth forth death.
—JAMES 1:14–15

The mother of harlots seduces and enslaves men and women because of the idols of their heart and fleshly lusts that war against their soul.

For all that is in the world, the lust of the flesh, and the lust of the eyes, and the pride of life, is not of the Father, but is of the world.

—1 JOHN 2:16, KJV

What the world has to offer is essentially the love of money, covetousness, which is idolatry, and the works of the flesh. A man will worship what he treasures in his heart and what he has an appetite for. If money or sexual perversion is what he treasures, these are the idols he would worship.

> With much justifying and enticing argument she persuades him, with the allurements of her lips she leads him [to overcome his conscience and his fears] and forces him along.
>
> Suddenly he [yields and] follows her reluctantly like an ox moving to the slaughter, like one in fetters going to the correction [to be given] to a fool or like a dog enticed by food to the muzzle.
>
> Till a dart [of passion] pierces and inflames his vitals; then like a bird fluttering straight into the net [he hastens], not knowing that it will cost him his life.
>
> Listen to me now therefore, O you sons, and be attentive to the words of my mouth.
>
> Let not your heart incline toward her ways, do not stray into her paths.
>
> For she has cast down many wounded; indeed, all her slain are a mighty host.
>
> Her house is the way to Sheol (Hades, the place of the dead), going down to the chambers of death.
>
> —PROVERBS 7:21–27, AMP

The law states that for a marriage covenant to be legal and binding, the ceremony must be performed before a legally authorized person, and the couple must consummate the marriage. The act of consummation is the joining of the flesh by sexual intercourse. Then and only then are the man and his wife considered as one flesh.

On this premise we believe that if two people become one flesh after they have become intimate, this act of intimacy also determines that when a spouse goes outside of the marriage covenant and have sexual intercourse with another person, the erring spouse also becomes one flesh with another person. When the unfaithful spouse returns to the marriage bed and becomes intimate with the marriage partner again, the marriage bed becomes defiled because the spirit of harlotry has now been introduced into the union.

As sexual diseases are transferred from one sex partner to another, spirits are also transferred during sexual intercourse. Not only is the unfaithful spouse one with the spirit of harlotry, but also the sins, diseases, iniquities, soul ties, and other spirits from the other sexual partner's bloodline are transferred to the wife or husband. If the wife is nursing a baby and receives a transfer of spirits and iniquities from her husband, the nursing child will also received a transfer of everything that was transferred into the mother, and at a set time in that child's life, those hidden spirits and iniquities will manifest.

> Do you not discern and understand that you [the whole church at Corinth] are God's temple (His sanctuary), and that God's Spirit has His permanent dwelling in you [to be at home in you, collectively as a church and also individually]?
>
> If anyone does hurt to God's temple or corrupts it [with false doctrines] or destroys it, God will do hurt to him and bring him to the corruption of death and destroy him. For the temple of God is holy (sacred to Him) and that [temple] you [the believing church and its individual believers] are.
>
> —1 Corinthians 3:16–17

When a man joins himself to a prostitute, he becomes one body with her. The two, as it is written, shall become one flesh. Similarly, when a woman joins herself to a man that is a whoremonger, they become one flesh, and that spirit will be transferred to her. All their sexual partners will receive the diseases, the bondages, habits, and curses associated with that unclean spirit of whoredom.

> Do you not see and know that your bodies are members (bodily parts) of Christ (the Messiah)? Am I therefore to take the parts of Christ and make [them] parts of a prostitute? Never! Never!
>
> Or do you not know and realize that when a man joins himself to a prostitute, he becomes one body with her? The two, it is written, shall become one flesh.
>
> But the person who is united to the Lord becomes one spirit with Him.
>
> —1 Corinthians 6:15–17

> Let marriage be held in honor (esteemed worthy, precious, of great price, and especially dear) in all things. And thus let the marriage bed be undefiled (kept undishonored); for God will judge and punish the unchaste [all guilty of sexual vice] and adulterous.
>
> —Hebrews 13:4

The Holy Spirit will not be in a marriage bed that is defiled by the spirit of harlotry. The Holy Spirit operating under the power of agreement is in the midst when the man and his wife are intimate with each other because the Holy Spirit abides within the reborn human spirit. Therefore, intimacy is not just between the man of God and the woman of God, but they are being intimate with the Holy Spirit in the bond of matrimony, honoring God with their sex life, which is a form of worship. The law of agreement says if two on earth shall agree, God is in the midst of the agreement, which is why it is important that married partners honor each other and speak words of blessing to each other.

Her Weapons of War

Flirtation and flattery

> For the commandment is a lamp; and the law is light; and reproofs of instruction are the way of life: to keep thee from the evil woman, from the flattery of the tongue of a strange woman.
>
> —Proverbs 6:23–24, kjv

> Say to skillful and godly Wisdom, You are my sister, and regard understanding or insight as your intimate friend.
>
> That they may keep you from the loose woman, from the adventuress who flatters with and makes smooth her words.
>
> —Proverbs 7:4–5, amp

The spirit of harlotry is very subtle and has many ploys. A flirtatious spirit lusts after flesh. It is the same spirit that causes people to prowl on the Internet, looking for sexual encounters with minors and people they do not know.

Flirting is one of the ploys of the spirit of harlotry. Flirtation is seductive, and it is a pastime that is enjoyed by the people who have the characteristics of this spirit. They are flirtatious. They often would say, "I am not doing any harm. I am just paying the young woman or the man a compliment, or I am just telling him how good he looks." But what men and women who are flirtatious do not realize is that flirtation opens the door to other forms of sexual lusts and bondage, such as adultery, fornication, sodomy, pedophilia, pornography, incest, male and female prostitution, etc. When you flirt, you are sending a message that says, "I am available. I am lusting. I am willing to accommodate you. Try me."

Leslie is a young woman who was flirtatious. Her targets were older married men who always flirted with her. She took great delight in all the attention, overtures, and suggestions she was getting from these older men, and she spent a lot of time in their company. What started with one man eventually became a lifestyle she enjoyed. She flirted with all the men at her place of employment. She flirted with men she did not know on the streets. She would go to church to flirt with men. She loved and enjoyed how that spirit made her feel. She felt wanted and accepted because she suffered from the painful rejection of her family.

Her face would light up when a man paid her a compliment or attempted to have a conversation with her. But that spirit was attracting other contentious spirits to her. One day, two men pulled up beside her at the traffic light and began flirting with her. She rolled her window all the way down and responded. She was grinning from ear to ear, having fun as they followed her home. When she stopped her car and got out, the men stopped their car and got out also. Then she realized she had picked up trouble. She ran into the house as they attempted to come after her, but the presence of her father stopped them. They got back into their car and drove away. Many women have become victims of sexual predators and murderers who use flirtation to lure their victims.

Flattery and flirtation are a ploy of the mother of harlots because they weaken strong men and take into captivity silly woman. Flattery and flirtation have the element of seduction in them because they stroke the ego and cause adrenaline to be pumped into the body.

A true compliment is designed to make a person feel good about what they have accomplished. It highlights accomplishments and encourages the hearer to persevere. What is said, the hearer knows to be a fact, which causes the hearer to feel a sense of pride—not negative arrogance but pride in the fact that that person gave his or her all, and now he or she is experiencing success in their endeavors. It could be losing weight, starting a business, completing a degree program, or receiving a promotion on the job. Whatever the accomplishment, a compliment is supposed to inspire.

Witchcraft

In the Western world, the church seems to be ignorant of the true nature of witchcraft. Most Christians in churches in America cannot define or identify witchcraft when it is among them, and if they do, they go into hysteria. Witchcraft is sometimes subtle and is practiced by some of the nicest people you know. It has the element of manipulation, craftiness, and control and is camouflaged or wrapped in a beautiful package with a title. There is witchcraft in every segment of society, and many people involved in religion practice some form of it knowingly or ignorantly, especially people who are controlling and force their will on others. What they are doing is a form of witchcraft. Then there are those people in the church and self-proclaimed witches who practice iniquity by praying against the will of God for a person's life. This practice is called witchcraft.

Witchcraft, harlotry, adultery, and idolatry are one and the same spirit because the root is the same. The branches may be different in some respects, but they bear the same fruit. When anyone is stung by the spirit of witchcraft, they manifest certain symptoms. They become disoriented and confused. In that state, they are easy to control and to be used to the advantage of their captors.

Many men in leadership criticize Elijah, the prophet, for running away from the death threats of Jezebel, the queen of Israel, who was married to King Ahab. They see Jezebel as just a woman without understanding the intensity and the level of the spiritual battle that Elijah was engaged in.

To understand what was really going on in Israel, you have to perceive it from the realm of the spirit. Jezebel was not only a queen with authority over a nation, but Jezebel was also a witch of the highest order in the kingdom of darkness.

Unclean spirits or demons do not have genders; they are not male or female. They manifest in various forms: human, animal, or grotesque-looking creatures. They can also transform themselves into an angel of light. (See 2 Corinthians 11:14, NIV.) And no wonder, for Satan himself masquerades as an angel of light. They are entities that work through the body of any person who is willing to accommodate them.

On hearing that Elijah had killed the prophets of Baal, Jezebel had supernatural demonic power to conjure up many demons at her disposal to attack Elijah. What made Elijah run was the impact of the strongest sting of witchcraft that the enemy could hurl at any mortal man. Elijah was a principality in the kingdom of God, the Chariot of Israel (2 Kings 2:11–12), whereas Jezebel was a principality in the kingdom of darkness, a high priestess.

The bombardment from witchcraft powers was so strong that the heavy oppression of darkness made Elijah feel so depressed and discouraged that he wanted to die. He wanted to give up his ministry. It made Elijah feel alone, afraid, weary, and abandoned. It caused him to doubt and question his own calling and purpose. Under this type of attack, the humanity and weakness of mortal flesh felt the weight of his responsibilities, and Elijah said, "It is too much for me," and this mighty warrior asked God to take his life. (See 1 Kings 19:4.)

We are living in the last days in which the powers of darkness are operating on the highest level of astrometaphysical consciousness in every realm of the material world. These powers are always looking for manifestation in the material world in order for them to operate, occupy, and take dominion. All they need is someone to agree with them in the earth realm to bring their ideologies and craft into manifestation. God told the children of Israel, "You shall not allow a woman to live who practices sorcery" (Exod. 22:18).

The legal doorway for any human being to come into the earth realm is through a womb. Satan and his hordes of evil spirits cannot use this doorway, but they can operate in the earth by affiliating themselves with mankind. The rate of acceleration of wickedness and evil in the material world is due to the degree of unrighteousness and abominations prevailing among men. These wicked spirits form alliances with wicked people with whom they have an ally, and a channel through which they can carry out their diabolical works. These diabolical activities are carried out by a network of spirits and human agents through such means as fortune-telling, horoscope, the area of parapsychology [telepathy, clairvoyance, and extrasensory perception], physiognomy, palmistry, shadow reading, and different forms of divination, which are specific channels of psychic enslavement leading people blindly to the path of witchcraft.

> There shall not be found among you any one that maketh his son or his daughter to pass through the fire, or that useth divination, or an observer of times, or an enchanter, or a witch, or a charmer, or a consulter with familiar spirits, or a wizard, or a necromancer. For all that do these things are an abomination unto the Lord; and because of these abominations the Lord thy God doth drive them out from before you.
>
> —Deuteronomy 18:10–12

Idolatry

Idolatry is witchcraft. It was the root cause of Israel's estrangement from God. The children of Israel did not know what Yahweh looked like, so they copied the practices of the heathen nations around them. These pagan nations believed that the worship of several gods was superior to the worship of a single God. Israel was fascinated with the forms of religious practices and worship of these deities, which were replicas of demonic principalities. Israel was influenced by the heathen nation's religious culture and constantly imitated them by worshiping their gods. This sin reoccurred throughout the history of Israel and caused God to be angry with them constantly. God allowed their enemies to gain control over them until finally, God's patience ran out and He allowed the Assyrians to destroy Israel's capital and to scatter the ten tribes. (See 2 Kings 17:6–18.)

The southern kingdom of Judah did have some God-fearing kings, such as Josiah, Hezekiah, and Jehoshaphat, but the wicked kings like Manasseh caused idolatry to be so embedded into the heart and lifestyles of the nation (2 Kings 21:1–9) that, as a result, God allowed Jerusalem to be destroyed and His people to go into exile for seventy years. The period of the seventy-year captivity broke the people's association with the idols of Canaan, and when the Jews later returned from captivity, idolatry ceased to be a major problem.

What is idolatry?

Idolatry can be described as image worship or divine worship given to an image of a heathen god, which, in reality, is demon worship. It is divine significance given to various forms and shapes.

Idolatry embodies a false notion of God. The heathen worshiped idols of war, love, death, passion, wickedness, lust, corruption, fertility, etc.

> I am the LORD thy God, which have bought thee out of the land of Egypt, out of the house of bondage. Thou shalt have no other gods before me. Thou shalt not make unto thee any graven image, or any likeness of any thing that is in heaven above, or that is in the earth beneath, or that is in the water under the earth. Thou shalt not bow down thyself to them, nor serve them; for I the LORD thy God, am a jealous God, visiting the iniquity of the fathers upon the children unto the third and fourth generation of them that hate me.
>
> —Exodus 20:2–5

Idols of the heart

> Stubbornness is as idolatry.
>
> —1 SAMUEL 15:23

> The works of the flesh are manifest, which are these…idolatry, witch-craft, hatred, variance…
>
> —GALATIANS 5:19–20

> Covetousness…is idolatry.
>
> —COLOSSIANS 3:5

> And the word of the LORD came unto me, saying, Son of man, these men have set up their idols in their heart, and put the stumblingblock of their iniquity before their face: should I be enquired of at all by them?
>
> Therefore speak unto them, and say unto them, Thus saith the Lord GOD; Every man of the house of Israel that setteth up his idols in his heart, and putteth the stumblingblock of his iniquity before his face, and cometh to the prophet; I the LORD will answer him that cometh according to the multitude of his idols.
>
> —EZEKIEL 14:2–4, KJV

The true nature of idolatry

The true nature of idolatry is demon worship. The worshipers felt that the powers behind the idols were able to impart temporary material and physical benefits to them. Some of these benefits were attractive to the Israelites, as they are to people today. Furthermore, the pagan gods did not require the kind of obedience that the God of Israel demanded.

Many pagan religions included sexual immorality with temple prostitutes as part of their religious rituals. This practice appealed to many Israelite men. But Jehovah required a higher moral standard for His people to maintain a relationship with Him.

> Now these things occurred as examples to keep us from setting our hearts on evil things as they did. Do not be idolaters, as some of them were, as it is written the people sat down to eat and drink and got up to indulge in pagan revelry. We should not commit sexual immorality, as some of them did—and in one day twenty-three thousand of them died.
>
> —1 CORINTHIANS 10:6–8, NIV

A perfect example was Eli, the high priest whose two sons, Hophni and Phinehas, were guilty of committing adultery with the women at the door of the temple. As part of their worship to their god Baal, pagan women came to the door of the tabernacle of Moses. Their worship involved ritualistic sex. They presented themselves at the door of the tabernacle to ensnare the Hebrew men that came there to worship Jehovah and to entice the priests and Levites who served and worked at the tabernacle to join them in the worship of Baal, which involved sex. Sex is as much a spiritual mystery as physical fact. Through sex the men, who were leaders and fathers in Israel, would be joined to another spirit entity.

> While Israel was staying in Shittim, the men began to indulge in sexual immorality with Moabite women, who invited them to the sacrifices to their gods. The people ate and bowed down before these gods. So Israel joined in worshipping the Baal of Peor. And the Lord's anger burned against them.
>
> —NUMBERS 25:1–3, NIV

> Now Eli was very old, and heard all that his sons did unto all Israel; and how they lay with the women that assembled at the door of the tabernacle of the congregation.
>
> —1 SAMUEL 2:22, KJV

Today, idolatry is found whenever or wherever people give themselves over to greed and materialism. It is found within the congregation of believers who claim to serve God and experience His salvation yet still participate in immorality and wickedness.

King Saul went to the witch at Endor, but he could not go in his capacity as king. He had to disguise himself by removing his kingly robes. Pretending to be someone else, he put on other garments as a disguise and submitted himself to the ministry of a witch. This practice was outlawed in Israel by God and reinforced by Saul. But Saul was a prideful man who was disobedient and rebellious. Samuel the prophet was dead, and because of Saul's disobedience, God was no longer on speaking terms with Saul. Saul turned to a witch for counsel and guidance, but despite his disguise, the witch was able to identify who he was. She cried out, "Why have you deceived me? For you are Saul" (1 Sam. 28:12).

Then Saul said to his servants, Find me a woman who is a medium [between the living and the dead], that I may go and inquire of her. His servants said, Behold, there is a woman who is a medium at Endor.

So Saul disguised himself, put on other raiment, and he and two men with him went and came to the woman at night. He said to her, Perceive for me by the familiar spirit and bring up for me the dead person whom I shall name to you.

The woman said, See here, you know what Saul has done, how he has cut off those who are mediums and wizards out of the land. Why then do you lay a trap for my life to cause my death?

And Saul swore to her by the Lord, saying, As the Lord lives, there shall no punishment come to you for this.

The woman said, Whom shall I bring up for you? He said, Bring up Samuel for me.

And when the woman saw Samuel, she screamed and she said to Saul, Why have you deceived me? For you are Saul!

—1 Samuel 28:7–12

Under the New Testament covenant, true Christians are not to seek counsel or direction from witches or psychics. When the people of God take off their spiritual garments (their robe of righteousness and their garment of praise) and put on other raiment as a disguise to commit iniquity and to live in sin, they can still be identified by God and the powers of darkness.

When true sons of God submit themselves to an idolatrous lifestyle, they give Satan, who is the accuser of the brethren, a legitimate case to file charges against them in the courts of heaven. God has a judicial system. Jesus is our advocate and defense attorney. When Satan brings a case before the judgment seat of God, it is because he knows that this child of God has committed iniquity, because the temptation and the assignment came from him. But thank God, the blood of Jesus was placed on the mercy seat in the place of judgment, and it is there to remind the devil that man's redemption has been paid and we can be acquitted from guilt.

HER ASSIGNMENT AGAINST VIRGINS

Do you not know that your body is the temple (the very sanctuary) of the Holy Spirit Who lives within you, Whom you have received [as a Gift] from God? You are not your own,

> You were bought with a price [purchased with a preciousness and paid for, made His own]. So then, honor God and bring glory to Him in your body.
>
> —1 CORINTHIANS 6:19–20

A virgin is a woman or man who has never had sexual intercourse, one who is chaste, modest, untouched, unmarked, pure, clean, undiscovered, and unused. Virginity is also a spiritual condition.

The spirit of harlotry has an assignment against all virgins because of the purity and singleness of a virgin's body (temple). A virgin is not only pure in body but also pure in spirit, which makes the body holy. When the body is holy, it can become an abiding place for the Holy Spirit. This is the reason for acts of sexual violence against children, to defile and contaminate that which is pure and innocent, and to deface the image of God the Father in young children. The assignment against virgins is to contaminate the temple by sexual abuse.

> And He called a little child to Himself and put him in the midst of them, and said, Truly I say to you, unless you repent (change, turn about) and become like little children [trusting, lowly, loving, forgiving], you can never enter the kingdom of heaven [at all].
>
> Whoever will humble himself therefore and become like this little child [trusting, lowly, loving, forgiving] is greatest in the kingdom of heaven.
>
> And whoever receives and accepts and welcomes one little child like this for My sake and in My name receives and accepts and welcomes Me.
>
> But whoever causes one of these little ones who believe in and acknowledge and cleave to Me to stumble and sin [that is, who entices him or hinders him in right conduct or thought], it would be better (more expedient and profitable or advantageous) for him to have a great millstone fastened around his neck and to be sunk in the depth of the sea.
>
> —MATTHEW 18:2–6

Pedophiles are people used by the mother of harlots to rape and sexually molest children. If the predator is a family member, then the crime committed is incest. This act of violence against children is deemed by the kingdom of darkness as putting a satanic mark on a child, a family, or a generation.

Boys who have been sexually molested may hate sodomy and the lifestyle that goes with it, but when a young man has lost his virginity through sexual molestation, a spirit of perversion lodges in his soul. The soul is the seat of the personality, the mind, will, intellect, and emotions. When a spirit of perversion has its habitation in a person's soul, these very powerful spirits can alter the personality and even the physical appearance of their victim.

The mind is the gateway to the soul. These spirits can alter a person's thought patterns, their mannerisms, perception of themselves, their will, and their emotions. They will flash images of sexual encounters in the person's mind, relentlessly bombarding their thoughts and imaginations with perversion, pornographic images, and overwhelming sexual suggestions.

People who do not have the power of the Holy Spirit and do not know about spiritual warfare and the battlefield of the mind are easy targets. When they accept these images, imaginations, and thoughts as their own; believe that this is who they are; and begin to identify with the spirit's thought patterns and suggestions, they form an emotional bond with the spirit entity, which we call a soul tie. This makes it easy for them to have alternative lifestyle opportunities and encounters that will determine their identity and destiny.

Another weapon the spirit of harlotry uses against women is rape. A young woman who has been raped or sexually molested may suffer from the shame of it for many years. That young lady may marry someday, but without therapy, she may have problems with her sexual performance. If she never dealt with the issues that affected her soul because of the impact of that negative encounter, she would be frigid, angry, ashamed, and experience bouts of rage because she is unable to respond to the sexual advances of her husband, which will cause problems in the marriage, such as infidelity or divorce.

Some women have been so demoralized by rape and repeated molestation, especially if the perpetrator was a family member or close family friend, that they become promiscuous. The impact of their ordeal has caused them to lose their self-worth. They could never have a relationship with a man without engaging in sex, because their thinking has become so warped that they believe in their hearts that sex is love, and what they want most of all is someone to love them.

The carnal man does not understand spiritual things. Some do not believe in Satan or God, and they dismiss the notion that there is a kingdom of darkness where Satan rules. To tell them that they are controlled by spiritual powers of darkness would be completely absurd. In their foolish pride they accept the notion that their level of education and their field of endeavor make them knowledgeable of all things both natural and spiritual. But what they fail to understand is that their unbelief does not negate the fact that there is a God and there is a prince of darkness called by several names, one of which is Satan.

Satan is a master strategist who controls behavior and the lifestyle choices of people by planting thoughts, ideas, and suggestions in the mind of people. Every wicked and immoral act against mankind began with a thought. After he has planted the thought, he follows through with the temptation. When the temptation is accepted and conceived, he follows through by persuading his victims to put their thoughts into action. All behavior stems out of a belief system, and people will always act on what they believe. For as a man thinks in his heart so is he.

Through association, all people who subscribe to a particular philosophy or concept become a part of a company or body of people who practice what they believe. To be a part of that company, one also has to believe that this particular philosophy and preceding behavior is right or represents truth. It may be organized religion, with rules that determine lifestyle and acceptable behavior, or an unorganized group of people who subscribe to deviant, sexual behavior. The gay movement or the homosexual lifestyle is not something that is new. Sexual deviance dates back to ancient biblical times. We first heard of sodomy when the Bible tells us the story of God's judgment against the cities of Sodom and Gomorrah.

As an educated society, we know that nobody is born gay. There is no such thing as a gay baby. When a child is born, it is identified as either male or female because there is no such thing as gay genitals. But life is all about choices, as we believe and think. We choose to practice and live accordingly, and Satan knows the power of the mind, for it is the doorway to the soul.

Most people do not know or understand how sexually deviant behavior can keep them in a life of bondage and slavery to the powers of darkness. Churches are mandated through the Word of God to preach a message of abstinence as a requisite for unmarried Christians. Satan hates and abhors virgins, because a sanctified body is the temple of God. Demons spirits are transferred into the temple of God through illicit sex, and the spirit of harlotry in her warfare against virgins assigns predators to soil the purity of virgins and to desecrate their temple. This is the reason behind the rise in immoral sexual attacks against children.

When a chosen one (male or female) loses their virginity outside of the marriage covenant, this causes great rejoicing in the demonic realm, especially if the chosen one brings forth seed out of wedlock. The mother of harlots tries to sabotage the life of chosen ones at an early age so that the preacher of righteousness would not come forth. Her plan is to capture a generation of young people by bringing them into bondage with sexual lust and perversion, which diminishes and aborts the anointing on their life. Sexual lust hinders movement toward God-ordained destiny.

There are so many tares (children of darkness) in the house of God. They have a form of godliness but not a relationship with the true and living God. They have come to the house of God seeking relationship with the children of God, and many of them are there to persuade the called ones who are not grounded in the Word to have relationship without commitment and sex outside of marriage.

When a virgin falls into the trap of the mother of harlots, Satan, who is the accuser of the brethren (the prosecuting attorney), can now go before God and plead his case against that person, even though he orchestrated the temptation, set the traps, created the environment, assigned his demons, and chose his victims.

When a minister falls into sexual sin, he or she loses credibility because Satan wants to attach a stigma of shame to the life of the man or woman of God; and no matter how God uses them, that stigma will follow the servant of God throughout their life and ministry. He will be known for his transgressions, no matter how many years have gone by. Even though God forgives, restores, and life goes on, God gets no glory out of our disobedience and waywardness, so He warns us to flee fornication.

> There hath no temptation taken you but such as is common to man: but God is faithful, who will not suffer you to be tempted above that ye are able; but will with the temptation also make a way to escape, that ye may be able to bear it.
>
> —1 Corinthians 10:13, kjv

> Let no one say when he is tempted, I am tempted from God; for God is incapable of being tempted by [what is] evil and He Himself tempts no one.

But every person is tempted when he is drawn away, enticed and baited by his own evil desire (lust, passions).

Then the evil desire, when it has conceived, gives birth to sin, and sin, when it is fully matured, brings forth death.

—JAMES 1:13–15

If we [freely] admit that we have sinned and confess our sins, He is faithful and just (true to His own nature and promises) and will forgive our sins [dismiss our lawlessness] and [continuously] cleanse us from all unrighteousness [everything not in conformity to His will in purpose, thought, and action].

—1 JOHN 1:9

SPIRIT WIVES AND SPIRIT HUSBANDS

Because sexual promiscuity is so blatant and widespread in our culture, the problem of spirit wives or spirit husbands is universal. The church has not yet come to the realization of the degree to which this phenomenon exists and many are too ashamed to ask for help. A demon that sexually attacks women is called an incubus and one that concentrates on men is called a succubus.

The sons of God saw that the daughters of men were fair, and they took wives of all they desired and chose....

There were giants on the earth in those days—and also afterward—when the sons of God lived with the daughters of men, and they bore children to them. These were the mighty men who were of old, men of renown.

—GENESIS 6:2, 4

Incubi and succubi are spirits with a sexual appetite. They come to people to inflame their sexual passion, to molest, torment, and abuse them sexually. Some of them unwittingly marry their victims in a dream. These demons (incubi and succubi) are so powerful that once they have taken someone for their wife or husband, they become very jealous. They are jealous to the point that if the woman gets pregnant in the natural, they try to kill the woman during childbirth or never allow the woman to give birth in natural life. Women who are victims of spirit husbands find it very difficult to get married in the natural. In fact, the spirit husband will be so angry that he will attempt to deal with anyone who tries to share his wife with him.

Succubi can also be wicked human spirits or satanic agents who level their power against another person. Any satanic agent, whether male or female, can become your spirit husband or spirit wife, chiefly because in real life they have found someone they admire, and they have used their evil powers to get what they want from their unsuspecting victims. This is done by the transference of their spirit out of their body and assuming the appearance of someone familiar before engaging in sex with their victim.

They put on the appearance of a respected friend, a pastor, or any person who is respected or admired, in order not to attract suspicion or resistance. Manifesting as a total stranger will no doubt result in resistance. When these wicked human spirits have sex with their victim, they also transfer their evil deposits. Women molested by these spirits always have problems with their female organs. There are men who are not practicing the same-sex lifestyle but are tormented by these spirits at night.

Satan has his own harem of women (concubines) in the church who will never be married in the natural because they are already married in the spirit. These women are gullible because they are lonely and emotionally weak. You will often hear them saying, "God said I am going to marry Pastor so-and-so." What is amazing about this is that groups of these women all claim that God told them to marry the same man. This is out of character for God. He does not play foolish games like that with His children. This deception is widespread in the church, and this spirit is so subtle that it makes women or men believe that they have heard from God. They put their life, their ministry, their goals, their dreams, and their vision on hold, wasting time waiting for this person to marry them in the natural, not understanding that this is a spiritual phenomenon. The enemy has enticed them, captured them through their lusts and vain imaginations, and turned them over to the keeper of the women, into the custody of Shaashgaz.

Because they are caught up in this deception, some of these women are victims of spirits who molest them at night, who impersonate the men they are waiting to marry. It does not matter how many eligible men approach these women to have a meaningful relationship. They will ignore their advances and eventually run them off.

If anyone is consciously or unconsciously married in the spirit realm, that person has a big problem because a spirit marriage is just as binding as a physical one, and the spirit spouse would fight to the end to keep his or her partner, even if it means killing their physical spouse if he or she gets in the way. Dreams of having sex or getting married in the spirit should be taken seriously. Aggressive prayers for deliverance to destroy and paralyze these strongmen must be made.

The law of yielding and bondage states that you will become a servant or slave to whatever you yield yourself to and are overcome by, whether it is narcotics, cigarettes, alcohol, food, sexual addiction, lying, etc. Whatever you are addicted to becomes your master.

> Do you not know that if you continually surrender yourselves to anyone to do his will, you are the slaves of him whom you obey, whether that be to sin, which leads to death, or to obedience which leads to righteousness (right doing and right standing with God)?
> —Romans 6:16

> Let no one say when he is tempted, I am tempted from God; for God is incapable of being tempted by [what is] evil and He Himself tempts no one.
> But every person is tempted when he is drawn away, enticed and baited by his own evil desire (lust, passions).
> Then the evil desire, when it has conceived, gives birth to sin, and sin, when it is fully matured, brings forth death.
> —James 1:13–15

But when a person yields to and is overcome by spirits of sexual perversion, and they begin to engage in sex with multiple sexual partners and to participate in orgies, prostitution, pedophilia, and pornography, this triggers a manifestation from the spirit realm. They have become one with a demonic entity. These spirits will keep their victims on a leash, constantly driving them as their slave to do things that are abnormal, animalistic, and depraved. The driving force is the insatiable appetite of the flesh, which the spirit enflames with unbridled passion. This is the power and purpose behind spirit wives, spirit husbands, and people who are sexual perverts.

Many people who have been exposed to the Word of God and realize they have a spirit of perversion or serpentine spirit in their life seek God for deliverance. By the Word of God they instinctively know that their behavior is unusual because a spirit other than the Holy Spirit of God controls their sexual behavior.

Chapter 5

DIVORCE AND REMARRIAGE

For the Lord, the God of Israel, says: I hate divorce and marital separation and him who covers his garment [his wife] with violence. Therefore keep a watch upon your spirit [that it may be controlled by My Spirit], that you deal not treacherously and faithlessly [with your marriage mate].

—MALACHI 2:16

T HE CHURCH IS EXPERIENCING AN UNPRECEDENTED RATE OF DIVORCE, and it is happening in religious institutions that in previous years had written in their constitution a clause pertaining to the evil of divorce. They have now slackened the rules and made amendments to their constitution to give men of rank in the body of Christ the opportunity to divorce their wives without retaliation from the governing board of elders. This action has opened a major door. When the custodians of the law break the law and break God's heart concerning the family, their action disqualifies them from teaching God's people about the sanctity of the marriage covenant. This evil perpetuates itself into the next generation of children who are affected by the selfishness of their parents.

Apostles, bishops, pastors, and elders make up the governing body of the church. They interpret the Word of God for the people, and they are responsible for adhering to and promulgating the principles and doctrinal standards of the faith. But due to their unfaithfulness to their covenant with God and their clandestine affairs and lifestyle, they have put a question mark in the minds of the next generation on the sanctity of marriage. To further the church's dilemma, some denominations have begun confirming people with an alternate lifestyle to stand in the pulpit as God's representatives, His voice to the people. The church has given them license and authority to speak to the body of believers on behalf of God.

For this august body of ministers, marriage is a moral issue. Some have chosen to remain celibate; others have chosen to be married because it is better to marry than to be consumed with sexual lust. Marriage is honorable because it is a divine institution for the morally conscious. If God made everything good, unfaithfulness to one's spouse and divorce is not a part of God's original design. The problem lies within the inner sanctum of a person's heart.

> The heart is deceitful above all things, and it is exceedingly perverse and corrupt and severely, mortally sick! Who can know it [perceive, understand, be acquainted with his own heart and mind]?
>
> I the Lord search the mind, I try the heart, even to give to every man according to his ways, according to the fruit of his doings.
>
> —Jeremiah 17:9–10

Jesus reiterated, "Because of the hardness of man's heart Moses allowed them to divorce their wives, but from the beginning it was not so" (Matt. 19:8). Therefore, divorce is a heart issue. Jesus used the word *hardness* as it relates to stubbornness, indifference, disobedience, rebellion, selfishness, conceit, and unforgiveness. These are the seeds of divorce, and our children are the ones reaping the bitter fruit.

> And Pharisees came to Him and put Him to the test by asking, Is it lawful and right to dismiss and repudiate and divorce one's wife for any and every cause?
>
> He replied, Have you never read that He Who made them from the beginning made them male and female, and said, For this reason a man shall leave his father and mother and shall be united firmly (joined inseparably) to his wife, and the two shall become one flesh?
>
> So they are no longer two, but one flesh. What therefore God has joined together, let not man put asunder (separate).
>
> They said to Him, Why then did Moses command [us] to give a certificate of divorce and thus to dismiss and repudiate a wife?
>
> He said to them, Because of the hardness (stubbornness and perversity) of your hearts Moses permitted you to dismiss and repudiate and divorce your wives; but from the beginning it has not been so [ordained].
>
> —Matthew 19:3–8

What is adultery? It is the unlawful intercourse with the spouse of another. Adultery is both physical and spiritual. It is used to describe the transfer of affections from a marriage partner to another person. And, as in the case of Israel, it was the breach of their relationship with God through their idolatry, which was described as adultery or harlotry.

Jesus explained the nature of the sin of adultery, that it was a condition of the heart. It begins in the heart and becomes a heart condition before it manifests itself as a physical act.

> Ye have heard that it was said by them of old time, Thou shalt not commit adultery: But I say unto you, That whosoever looketh on a woman to lust after her hath committed adultery with her already in his heart...It hath been said, Whosoever shall put away his wife, let him give her a writing of divorcement: But I say unto you, That whosoever shall put away his wife, saving for the cause of fornication, causeth her to commit adultery: and whosoever shall marry her that is divorced committeth adultery.
>
> —MATTHEW 5:27–28, 31–32

BIBLICAL GROUNDS FOR DIVORCE

> Let marriage be held in honor (esteemed worthy, precious, of great price, and especially dear) in all things. And thus let the marriage bed be undefiled (kept undishonored); for God will judge and punish the unchaste [all guilty of sexual vice] and adulterous.
>
> —HEBREWS 13:4

Infidelity

What is infidelity? It is unfaithfulness, a lack of loyalty, a disloyal act, or adultery. When a married person violates the covenant and has sex outside of the marriage, not only is there unfaithfulness, sexual immorality, and betrayal, but it is also a violation against the Word of God to bring a third person into a one-flesh union. Married people are joined together by covenant. Infidelity is defilement of the marriage bed and is grounds for Christians to divorce. This rule applies not only to the Christian but also to the unsaved because infidelity not only defiles the marriage bed but it also causes a legal breach of the covenant.

Israel's unfaithfulness to God was spiritual adultery or harlotry because Israel had the propensity to worship a plethora of idols. They served other gods along with Jehovah (the true and living God), whom they were in covenant with, and who gave them laws to govern their spiritual, moral, and national life. One of those laws specifically stated, "And you shall love the Lord your God with all your [mind and] heart and with your entire being and with all your might" (Deut. 6:5). By breaking this covenant, Israel was considered as a wife of whoredom, an adulteress. The same charge is given to one who is married and is sexually immoral.

God used the relationship between the prophet Hosea and his wife, Gomer, who was a prostitute, as an allegory to state His case for His devotion and love toward his wife, Israel. Gomer was a slave to whoredom (sexual sins), yet her husband, the prophet and the man of God, was devoted to her despite her whoredom, her defilement of the marriage bed, and their estrangement. He bought her back from the flesh markets where she was being sold as a slave.

> The beginning of the word of the LORD by Hosea. And the Lord said to Hosea, Go, take unto thee a wife of whoredoms and children of whoredoms: for the land hath committed great whoredom, departing from the LORD.
>
> So he went and took Gomer the daughter of Diblaim; which conceived, and bare him a son....
>
> And she conceived again, and bare a daughter. And God said unto him, Call her name Loruhamah: for I will no more have mercy upon the house of Israel; but I will utterly take them away.
>
> —HOSEA 1:2–3, 6, KJV

> Plead with your mother, plead: for she is not my wife, neither am I her husband: let her therefore put away her whoredoms out of her sight, and her adulteries from between her breasts... And I will not have mercy upon her children; for they be the children of whoredoms. For their mother hath played the harlot: she that conceived them hath done shamefully: for she said, I will go after my lovers, that give me my bread and my water, my wool and my flax, mine oil and my drink...And she shall follow after her lovers, but she shall not overtake them; and she shall seek them, but shall not find them: then shall she say, I will go and return to my first husband; for then was it better with me than now.
>
> —HOSEA 2:2, 4–5, 7

And I will betroth you to Me forever; yes, I will betroth you to Me in righteousness and justice, in steadfast love, and in mercy.

I will even betroth you to Me in stability and in faithfulness, and you shall know (recognize, be acquainted with, appreciate, give heed to, and cherish) the Lord.

—Hosea 2:19–20

Abandonment

Abandonment by an unbelieving spouse is grounds for Christian divorce. When there is a union between a believer and an unbeliever, if the unbeliever keeps the marriage bed undefiled and their sexual relationship pure from contamination by the spirit of harlotry, the Spirit of Christ who sanctifies the believer will sanctify the unbeliever in that union.

> But to the married people I give charge—not I but the Lord—that the wife is not to separate from her husband.
>
> But if she does [separate from and divorce him], let her remain single or else be reconciled to her husband. And [I charge] the husband [also] that he should not put away or divorce his wife.
>
> To the rest I declare—I, not the Lord [for Jesus did not discuss this]—that if any brother has a wife who does not believe [in Christ] and she consents to live with him, he should not leave or divorce her.
>
> And if any woman has an unbelieving husband and he consents to live with her, she should not leave or divorce him.
>
> For the unbelieving husband is set apart (separated, withdrawn from heathen contamination, and affiliated with the Christian people) by union with his consecrated (set-apart) wife, and the unbelieving wife is set apart and separated through union with her consecrated husband. Otherwise your children would be unclean (unblessed heathen, outside the Christian covenant), but as it is they are prepared for God [pure and clean].
>
> But if the unbelieving partner [actually] leaves, let him do so; in such [cases the remaining] brother or sister is not morally bound. But God has called us to peace.
>
> For, wife, how can you be sure of converting and saving your husband? Husband, how can you be sure of converting and saving your wife?

—1 Corinthians 7:10–16

Married people are yoked together in covenant. They are yoke fellows. A yoke fellow is a companion, partner, or associate, or a husband or wife. The definition of the word *yoke* can vary[1]:

- A wooden frame or bar with loops or bows at either end, fitted around the necks of a pair of oxen for harnessing them together

- A pair of animals harnessed together (a yoke of oxen)

- Any mark or symbol of bondage or servitude

- Something that binds, unites, or connects (e.g., the yoke of matrimony)

- The cross piece used to hold two parts together

- To join together in marriage

An example of being unequally yoked is light and darkness, truth and error. The Bible admonishes the sons of God not to be unequally yoked with unbelievers. We are spirit beings with the Spirit of Christ dwelling in us. If we are yoked to an unbeliever, we can be yoked to an unclean spirit, the wrong bloodline, people who are cursed, or people who already have a covenant with Satan and are the children of darkness.

> Do not be unequally yoked with unbelievers [do not make mismated alliances with them or come under a different yoke with them, inconsistent with your faith]. For what partnership have right living and right standing with God with iniquity and lawlessness? Or how can light have fellowship with darkness?
>
> What harmony can there be between Christ and Belial [the devil]? Or what has a believer in common with an unbeliever?
>
> What agreement [can there be between] a temple of God and idols? For we are the temple of the living God; even as God said, I will dwell in and with and among them and will walk in and with and among them, and I will be their God, and they shall be My people.
>
> So, come out from among [unbelievers], and separate (sever) yourselves from them, says the Lord, and touch not [any] unclean thing; then I will receive you kindly and treat you with favor, and I will be

a Father to you, and you shall be My sons and daughters, says the
Lord Almighty.

—2 CORINTHIANS 6:14–18

There are other areas for legitimacy in divorce that may not be mentioned
in the Scriptures, such as if the marriage and divorce occurred prior to conver-
sion. When a person becomes a new creation in Christ Jesus, God gives them
a new heart, and old things are passed away.

Also, when a dominant spouse with a hard heart takes out of the marriage
more than they have put in, this leaves the other partner with an empty heart.
Abusers are people with hard hearts who take out more than they are willing
to put in. God will not obligate anyone to remain in an abusive situation
if their life is in jeopardy. God replenishes what has been depleted through
abuse, lack of love, infidelity, mismanagement and abandonment.

God is able and has on many occasions brought restoration and resurrection
to relationships that were dead for many years. As new creations in Christ, we
can forgive to release the hurt and pain caused by abusers, even if they have
never acknowledged their wrongdoing and sought forgiveness from God and
the offended spouse.

> Then said the Lord to me, Go again, love [the same] woman [Gomer]
> who is beloved of a paramour and is an adulteress, even as the Lord
> loves the children of Israel, though they turn to other gods and love
> cakes of raisins [used in the sacrificial feasts in idol worship].
>
> So I bought her for fifteen pieces of silver and a homer and a half
> of barley [the price of a slave].
>
> And I said to her, You shall be [betrothed] to me for many days;
> you shall not play the harlot and you shall not belong to another man.
> So will I also be to you [until you have proved your loyalty to me and
> our marital relations may be resumed].
>
> —HOSEA 3:1–3

SUBMISSION AND EXPECTATIONS

Submission is that dreaded word that women strongly object to, for it has been
used by some men to take control and become a bully in their family without
respect for their wife's opinion or suggestions. It also becomes a dreaded word
when a woman knows that her husband is financially irresponsible, unwise,

unfaithful, and immature. Many women have outgrown their husbands spiritually, mentally, financially, and emotionally, which makes the relationship challenging because the woman is no longer dependent on her husband for emotional or financial support and affirmation.

> Submitting yourselves one to another in the fear of God. Wives, submit yourselves unto your own husbands, as unto the Lord. For the husband is the head of the wife, even as Christ is the head of the church: and he is the saviour of the body. Therefore as the church is subject unto Christ, so let the wives be to their own husbands in every thing.
> —Ephesians 5:21–24, kjv

This word in Ephesians 5 was designed to give the church an understanding of the basic family structure and order, which begins with marriage between a man and a woman. The man is to exemplify Christ in a committed covenant relationship with a woman, who is bone of his bone and flesh of his flesh. These guidelines are for the church, not for the unsaved. If we go back to Genesis and read about the descendents of Cain, we will see that they lived by a different set of rules because Cain, along with his descendants, lived outside of the presence of God. We should not expect people who live outside of the presence of God to live according to the Bible, because they have a different spirit and a different god.

> And Cain went out from the presence of the Lord, and dwelt in the land of Nod, on the east of Eden.
> —Genesis 4:16, kjv

> This is a great mystery: but I speak concerning Christ and the church.
> —Ephesians 5:32, kjv

Gender has nothing to do with righteousness; therefore, being male does not make a man a good father or a great husband. Being male just qualifies a man to be a seed donor. Gender identifies the type of human being, whether male or female, but character defines and determines who a person is from the inside out.

There are phases and stages to life as we evolve, grow, and acquire wisdom, knowledge, and understanding. The natural order is that we grow into what we shall eventually become, because life is a series of stages. We eventually arrive at a destination or dimension, a place of maturity set by God. Also, during our lifetime, we strive to acquire and accomplish the goals and dreams that we set for ourselves. We call this ambition. God has given to mankind natural talents, gifts, and skills for the journey of life, and He gives wisdom to those who ask for wisdom so we may accomplish those goals and dreams. But to those called and chosen of God, He not only sets the course, opens the doors, and gives directions to us at every stage of the journey, but He also takes responsibility for us arriving at our predetermined destinations on time.

Some students drop out of school, and some adults drop out of life. The prison system is filled with people who have dropped out of life. The admonition here is this: if we cease to pursue our goals and grow weary, we will never attain to our maximum potential. There are a lot of obstacles along the road called progress, and it is strewn with hurdles we have to overcome. Adversity is a catalyst for growth to some, but it can also be a means of destruction for others without God-given courage, strength, and determination to survive. One method of survival is staying in the press and associating ourselves with people who are pressing forward in the same direction as we are. One of life's lessons is that we are not independent of each other. A man cannot say that he does not need a woman. Nor can a woman say that she doesn't need a man. We all need to know when to submit and how to do it gracefully.

> Nevertheless, in [the plan of] the Lord and from His point of view woman is not apart from and independent of man, nor is man aloof from and independent of woman;
> For as woman was made from man, even so man is also born of woman; and all [whether male or female go forth] from God [as their Author].
> —1 Corinthians 11:11–12

Submission denotes yielding, surrendering, obedience, and meekness. It is the act of submitting something to another for decision or consideration.

Under the terms of the law of agreement, the parties involved in a dispute submit the matter to arbitration and agree to be bound by the decision.

A submissive person is one that has a tendency to submit without resistance, who is docile and yielding but not necessarily foolish or weak. Submission is not something that women do; it is something we all do based on circumstances. Here are some examples of submission:

- Children under the tutelage and authority of their parents have to submit.

- The biblical example of the centurion who wanted Jesus to come and heal his servants but told Jesus, "You don't have to come to my house, just speak the word, because I also have servants under me, and when I say to one come he comes and when I say another do this he does it." (See Matthew 8:8–9).

- There are terms and conditions of employment we must submit and adhere to if we want to be hired.

Therefore, submission is the act of yielding to the actions, power, and control of another, which carries with it the tendency of allowing oneself to be subjected to the treatment, analysis, opinion, judgment, and decision of another. We are constantly being evaluated by people in authority at our places of employment based on their point of view, their moral compass, and their attitude toward life in general. Whether the environment is good or bad, we submit even when we are poorly treated, have been passed over for advancement, or have been discriminated against. Why do we submit? There are bills to be paid and responsibilities to our family. Submission is not gender oriented; both male and female have to submit to each other.

Submission in the context of marriage is different because in marriage there should be no bosses, even though there are differences in personality. Marriage is about love, agreement, and relationship, a pattern of Christ and His church. The bond that holds marriage together is love, and as we become one flesh in an uncompromising and holy union, God says, "I am in the midst," and He is there because of the power of agreement. Only in the power of agreement can dominion and authority be exercised, because in the family we submit one to another in the fear of God.

There are things that men do that they are very good at and we respect and honor our men for their God-given ability as heads of the family. There are areas that women are gifted in and that they excel at. When the husband and the wife bring their gifts and individual anointing into the union and submit to each other in love, their respective areas of expertise and endowments will enhance each other and will also benefit the children. Our children are the beneficiaries of the combined gifts and anointing of each parent.

In like manner, you married women, be submissive to your own husbands [subordinate yourselves as being secondary to and dependent on them, and adapt yourselves to them], so that even if any do not obey the Word [of God], they may be won over not by discussion but by the [godly] lives of their wives.

—1 Peter 3:1

In the same way you married men should live considerately with [your wives], with an]intelligent recognition [of the marriage relation], honoring the woman as [physically] the weaker, but [realizing that you] are joint heirs of the grace (God's unmerited favor) of life, in order that your prayers may not be hindered and cut off. [Otherwise you cannot pray effectively.]

—1 Peter 3:7

Another word we need to consider is *expectation*. There are many women and men who are disappointed in their marriages because their chosen spouse did not meet their level of expectation. They are disappointed after years of devotion to a partner, who, in their estimation, never amounted to much. Their disappointment was followed by silence, anger, rage, hostility, unforgiveness, and divorce.

Disappointment is one of the reasons why so many couples become so hostile to each other after years of marriage. Their disappointment was caused by an illusion based on the hope of having someone who would fulfill their fantasy.

A dear sister in the Lord testified about her pent-up rage toward her husband. She was so mad with her husband that she searched the Scriptures diligently looking for a legal way to get out of the marriage without violating God's Word. Her husband was not an adulterer, but his pride, selfishness, immaturity, rebellion, and stubbornness caused him to walk off lucrative jobs when he could not have his way. His actions cost the family dearly. They experienced homelessness and poverty and were constantly moving before the landlord could throw them out.

When they got married, he was an exceedingly attractive, educated man who was quite ambitious. After years of rebellion, he had become a couch potato with a remote control in his hand, demanding attention and complaining about their lack of money. He refused to work long enough for the family to get out of debt, but he expected his wife to find a solution for the financial dilemma the family was experiencing. She was disgusted and disappointed because she was stuck with the financial and emotional burden of the family while he sat in front of the television day after day.

This was a man she once loved and to whom she had given all her youthful years. She said to me, "This is not the man I married." This woman never expected to be the sole provider for the family, but she was stuck in a relationship that was going nowhere. The relationship never produced the benefits and promises that she expected. Years after her marriage vow, she still loved him, but she was sad, resentful, angry, and disappointed. His refusal to commit his life to God only complicated matters because he did not believe in God or in the power of prayer.

The pattern we have for raising our family is based on how we were raised by our parents. Some get their direction and rules for raising the family from friends, other family members, and television. Somewhere in the dating phase of a relationship, if one will only listen and pay attention to the obvious hints, that potential partner will let you know who they really are. Love covers a multitude of sins and faults, until after the marriage has been consummated and reality steps in.

Somewhere in the complexity of the female brain is the idea that she can marry a man and then change him. That theory never works. Only God can change a man, or sometimes tragedy will force him to change his lifestyle. By the time he reaches the age where he wants to marry, he has already been programmed. If he was unfaithful in the relationship before marriage, he would be unfaithful after marriage, and the same goes for the woman because marriage does not change a person's heart or character; it only makes the relationship legal. If he or she did not want responsibilities and hated holding a job before marriage, the possibility exists that after the marriage things are not going to change.

A young couple may start off at the same mental, emotional, and spiritual level, but if the woman matures faster than the male and he remains dwarfed mentally, spiritually, and emotionally, he would frustrate the grace of God on the woman's life. In such cases, the wife will seem to be bossy and controlling to those who live outside of the home. But the underlying cause of her frustration will be the failure of the husband to assume his priestly role.

Another point to consider is that many men think that their role as protector and provider is based on whether he is the primary breadwinner. If he is not and the wife is, he may take a secondary role in the leadership of the family and allow his wife to have the dominant role in the family. However, this is not the order of God. Most women have issues with submission when the head of the household would not provide for the family but takes delight in being demanding and bossy. Every person, before they say, "I do," should ask themselves this question: what am I submitting myself to?

In this generation, the body of Christ has many women who are educated professionals, and entrepreneurs who earn a decent salary. They are not financially dependent on their husbands and do not have a need to marry someone to take care of them. What they are really looking for is true love and a faithful man who is committed to God and family. If these basic qualities are not there, then this question must be asked by the women: if I marry this man, what am I coming into agreement with?

A dear brother in the Lord who came from a strong Christian family with a spiritual heritage of ministers in every generation met a young lady at church who also had a spiritual heritage. Yet in her rebellion against God and disobedience to her Christian values and upbringing, she walked on the wild side of life, taking and selling drugs, which caused her to spend valuable time in and out of jail.

Her family thought it would be a great idea to bring these two together so that she would have a strong Christian man for a husband who would turn her life around. The young man in question was new to the community church when he was introduced to the young lady. He started dating her, they fell in love, and were married. She did quite well for a period of time, but she never gave up her ungodly friends. She continued her association with the same company of people who did drugs, walked on the wrong side of the law, and went to jail for their criminal activity. Her husband worked at night, so she frequently hung out with her friends at the clubs and bars.

God used a prophet to give her a strong word of warning, to which she paid no attention. Eventually she started participating with her friends in criminal activity and once more became addicted to cocaine. She was arrested and put back into jail because she was in violation of her parole.

Marriage did not change her. Going to church never changed her, even though she was blessed with a good husband and her family gave them a beautiful house as a wedding present. Even with the support of a church and two beautiful children, her desire for drugs, her worldly friends, and her appetite for the lifestyle on the streets never changed. She went off to jail, leaving her husband to raise their children. He was hurt and disappointed because he never expected his wife to go back to the life she had before he met her. He felt his love was strong enough to change her.

Financial empowerment has leveled the playing field for women, but financial freedom brings responsibilities. What has developed in society is a breed of women who try to pick up and buy men with their money. They try to buy love and give lots of gifts in return for affection, sex, and control. Women have become the hunters, and there are men who love to be hunted by women with financial resources. These women, like their male counterpart, try to control the relationship with sex and money (areas of weakness for men) and give gifts as rewards to hold the man until they find out he is cheating on them with another woman who is also giving him money.

When men submit to this type of arrangement, they are not walking in the will of God. These men cannot qualify as heads of households because they have submitted to an arrangement that is not in compliance with biblical principles. This new role of women caretakers has given rise to another scenario. We now have a generation of men who want their girlfriends and wives to take care of them like their mothers.

This spirit is also in the church, and it is not unusual to hear several women in the church say that God told them to marry the same man. God is not the author of confusion. Having a man is not a retirement plan, and wanting to get married for the wrong reasons is also not a secure plan. When we relate marriage to God's kingdom design and purpose, we understand God's Word that says, "He who finds a [true] wife finds a good thing and obtains favor from the Lord" (Prov. 18:22). It is within the marriage union that certain blessings are released.

The Strongman Called Strife

Hatred stirs up strife, but love covers all sins.

—Proverbs 10:12, nkjv

Strife breaks, nullifies, or suspends the power of agreement. Where there is strife, there is disorder and chaos. Strife is a spirit. It is a strongman demonic entity. Strife is a weapon in the arsenal of Satan. He uses it to divide and conquer nations, churches, households, businesses, marriages, and any community of people who are gathered together for a common purpose. The negative emotions emitted by strife can cause depression if marriage partners allow themselves to be affected by incidental hurts and unkind criticisms.

Strife causes walls and barriers to be put in place to keep out offending parties and individuals, and many of these walls and blockages eventually become generational if not resolved. These walls can separate family members for generations and prevent fellowship and reunions. Many family members die without resolving conflicts, yet there are some enemies you just cannot resolve conflicts with, because their deep-seated jealousy and hatred will always make you a target of criticism. You cannot choose the family you were born into, but you can make wise choices with friendships by upgrading to a new environment and spending more time with successful people who are not in competition with your success.

When strife is unleashed in a marriage, the power of agreement is nullified, and division, anarchy, violence, disorder, and destruction reign. On a national level, strife causes civil disobedience and lawlessness. Civil unrest can develop to the stage where a nation can experience civil war all because of warring factions within the nation. On a global level, political strife causes nations to engage in warfare. World War I and II began because of political strife. On a family level, covenants are broken and good family relationships are severed and destroyed forever because of strife.

Strife changes the atmosphere and produces a climate of competition, jealousy, envy, hatred, and vindictiveness. If strife is present in a church, there can be no true worship, because God, who is love, and the spirit of strife cannot operate in the same environment. Jesus says a house or a kingdom divided against itself cannot stand. (See Matthew 12:25.)

> Therefore if thou bring thy gift to the altar, and there rememberest that thy brother hath ought against thee; Leave there thy gift before the altar, and go thy way; first be reconciled to thy brother, and then come and offer thy gift.
> —MATTHEW 5:23–24

This strongman is always looking for manifestation. When he channels his thoughts to the mind of a person and the recipient comes into agreement by verbalizing his suggestions or by acting on the thoughts, imagery, or messages received, it gives the strongman license to create an atmosphere that can be manipulated and impacted by strife.

As long as strife is sustained in a home, church, or a community, it will produce a climate of chaos and warfare. In many neighborhoods and communities where there is much violence, divorce, drug infestation, and all types of criminal activity, that atmosphere is control by demonic entities, one of which is strife.

Atmosphere produces climate, and climate that is sustained produces strongholds. Strongholds produce culture. Strongholds are thoughts or belief systems that have become philosophies, doctrines, or dogmas that are part of the culture of a people or nation. There are strongholds and traditions in every group of our society. One family may have a religious culture and yet not have a relationship with God. That religious culture will produce a generational stronghold. If you marry into a religious family and you do not subscribe to the culture, practices, and values of that family, that religious spirit will always instigate and create tension to force you into submission.

It is to the benefit of the kingdom of darkness to bring another soul into bondage through religion and not into relationship with God. Religious wars have been fought throughout the centuries by nations, tribes, and families. Countries have been divided along religious lines. Elections are sometimes decided by a candidate's religion. People will commit murder in the name of religion. Religion and strife are two spirits that work hand in hand to cause chaos and division in any segment of society and war in every nation of the world.

FAMILY DYNAMICS

The western hemisphere, especially North America, is a melting pot of many cultures and people from various socioeconomic backgrounds, religions, and nations. Those born in the Western world sometimes subscribe to the fact that when one marries a person, one does not marry the in-laws. Some consider the in-laws as optional, but in-laws can be a tremendous blessing or they can be a dysfunctional thorn in the flesh.

Understanding family structure and dynamics is important if one wants to have a happy, stable marriage. One should investigate family roots, family diseases, family bondages, culture, religion, and all the things that love causes one to overlook, which will eventually affect your marriage and will manifest in your relationship after you say, "I do for better or for worse."

Women are more prone than men to be romantic and to ignore the warning signs, to get too deeply involved emotionally and financially before finding out who the man really is and what his real intentions are. Silly women who are desperate for romance have a tendency to believe everything a flirtatious charmer says without first evaluating him. But what women fail to understand is that women were programmed differently than men. If all a man wants out of a relationship is sex and money, whatever he does and says will lead to that end. If he is not in love with the woman, after he has achieved his goal, the relationship will take a downward slide because he has lost interest, and his attention will be drawn to someone else. Meanwhile, the woman would still be trying to maintain the relationship, hoping that through sex and gifts his heart and mind would be focused on her.

Family dynamics and culture should help couples to understand each other better because every generation and bloodline has its own issues. Many children have had issues with regard to their parents' presence or absence in the home and how their life has been affected because of divorce. This is not an indictment against parents, but we recognize the fact that parents are not perfect either. Maturity dictates that we try to get along and mature into healthy emotional and spiritual human beings despite our negative heritage and whether we are in the same home or community or are separated by many miles. We should try not to carry our family dysfunction into the next generation.

We have been molded into who we have become as adults based on our family dynamics, structure, and our environment. And some of us have had to let go of the crusty past to embrace the future. Otherwise, the past will control and overly influence us negatively in our present and future as we try to build and structure our own family relationships.

I was ministering with a young woman who was very beautiful, but she could not stay in a stable relationship because she would always burden her male friends with her constant complaints about her family. She had issues she would not let go of or confront, and as the years went by, even though she did not remain in contact with her family, her issues got bigger and bigger until she could not define what was truth or childhood fantasy. She just hated everyone in her family.

Sibling rivalry and jealousy had turned into a full-scale war, and she was the only participant. Everyone else except her had grown up, settled down, and moved to the next level. Then she met the man of her dreams and wanted to get married. He had a good relationship with his family and introduced her to them. Now it was her turn to introduce him to her family, and she could not do so because her past was her present and she was taking her present baggage into her future.

David Field authored a book called *Family Personalities*, in which he wrote about understanding your parents once you become an adult. He also gave us five personality traits found in families. The following is a condensed description of these traits.[2]

The bonding family: This family is a model of the balance between individuality and relationships. This family equips its children with a strong sense of identity and security and a capacity to relate to others. This family encourages its individual members to be all that they can be. They are not threatened by their differences.

The ruling family: This family has a tendency to be abrasive or insensitive in their relationships. The parents push their authority. Consequently, the children do not feel cared for, but they do know how to perform tasks.

The protecting family: Children in this family feel cared for, but often the parents do too much for them. Consequently the child is not allowed to develop a sense of personal confidence. The parents do not make him endure the consequences of his behavior.

The chaotic family: This family is disengaged from each other. Their knowledge of and interest in one another is limited. They are more like roommates than a family. Each individual looks out for number one. Caring for others is considered absurd or stupid, and children are neglected or abused.

The symbiotic family: Individuals in this family find it impossible to be self-directed, because individuality is seen as a lack of allegiance to the family. They are weak as individuals but strong as a group. Children feel smothered in the family and guilty if they want to leave. Survival in the family comes from the ability to conform to the norms, drive the same kind of car, embrace the same political views, and like the same food.

Family dynamics also include how the parents related to each other—which parent had the dominant personality, their communication skills, how they managed crisis in the family, their religious influence, their moral values, their parenting style, and their response to their environment all contributed to the way the children functioned as adults.

The Bible tells us about a man named Noah who was the only righteous man in his generation. It was a time of great prosperity when men built houses, married wives, raised their families, planted their vineyards, and conducted business. Yet wickedness and violence were so great in the earth that God regretted that He had made man. Noah's environment was saturated with evil, wicked people and their lawless lifestyle. But Noah found grace in the eyes of the Lord because he was the only man found by God to be righteous. He raised his three sons in this environment to be good men when all flesh had corrupted itself in the eyes of God, and there was widespread violence and evil everywhere.

> The Lord saw that the wickedness of man was great in the earth, and that every imagination and intention of all human thinking was only evil continually.
> And the Lord regretted that He had made man on the earth, and He was grieved at heart.
> So the Lord said, I will destroy, blot out, and wipe away mankind, whom I have created from the face of the ground—not only man, [but] the beasts and the creeping things and the birds of the air—for it grieves Me and makes Me regretful that I have made them.
> But Noah found grace (favor) in the eyes of the Lord.
> —Genesis 6:5–8

As you study the personality of a family, you will discover and understand more about family dynamics and how this important information will help a person to better understand the spiritual and moral values of their potential spouse. Iniquity and righteousness are generational. We say children are products of their environment, but children are also products of their parents even when a maternal parent is absent. Children suffer from bloodline curses passed onto them from their parents, but the power of the Lord can set them free.

Many spouses complain about the dreaded mother-in-law who is always portrayed as a meddlesome, controlling woman who does not want to let her son or daughter go or her children to grow up. She insists on giving advice when no one wants it and is always telling everybody what they should or should not do. This is not the case with every mother-in-law, but it is the accepted norm for most women with a dominating personality who has a son or daughter that has grown older physically, but who is still mentally and emotionally attached and dependent on their mother. This problem can also be spiritual.

There are parents who live their lives vicariously through their children. Whatever they missed out on in life they try to accomplish through their children. Women who were disappointed and betrayed by someone they loved, and those who have a root of bitterness and unforgiveness in them, will try to control their children's relationships because they are dealing with their own hurts and failures of the past. Mothers and fathers-in-law must be respected, but they must also know their place, the extent and limits of their involvement, and not try to usurp authority in their children's marriage, except in the case where the spouse is an abuser.

A man must leave his father and mother's house and cleave to his wife, meaning he must have his own house to raise his family, and he must put his relationship with his wife and children above all others. However, women need protection from abusive, controlling men. A source of protection is her family. She should, if she can, maintain good relationships with members of her family, and not try to disengage herself from them after she is married.

Chapter 6

HOW TO BECOME SINGLE
AFTER DIVORCE

So he who cohabits with his neighbor's wife [will be tortured with evil consequences and just retribution]; he who touches her shall not be innocent or go unpunished.

—**Proverbs 6:29**

INGLE REFERS TO ONE WHO IS NOT UNITED WITH OR ACCOMPANIED BY another. In this chapter, we will try to answer the questions that many people who have experienced divorce have asked. How does the flesh become single after being joined to another in matrimony? How does the body heal itself emotionally, physically, and spiritually after separation or divorce? How do you purge the spirit of former sexual partners out of your body?

The key is *abstinence*. The spiritual implication is the *Sabbath*. The word *Sabbath* is an Aramaic word that means to cease and desist.1 The Hebrew *shābath* (Shabbat) or Arab *sabata* means to intercept and interrupt.[2] The double *b* has an intensive force, which implies a complete cessation or making to cease. The idea is not that of relaxation of refreshment but cessation from activity.

Jesus Christ is the Lord of Sabaóth, which is a transliteration of a Hebrew word that denotes hosts or armies. A title used to designate Him as the One who is supreme over all the innumerable hosts of spiritual agencies, or of what is described as "the armies of heaven." Jesus, in His capacity as Lord of Sabaóth drove out demonic spirits, cleansed the leper, restored sight to the blind, and healed the sick on the Sabbath day because the observance of the Sabbath was a means to an end.

The Sabbath was a time of consecration, which was coeval with the Creation. God rested on the Sabbath day and honored that day. The word *day* is a period

133

of time, such as twenty-four hours or one thousand years. A day of visitation does not mean a twenty-four hour period but could be a season of visitation from the Lord of Sabaôth, which can be months in which a church can experience the tangible presence of the Lord. It can also be a season of consecration for the healing and restoration for an individual. To become single, one needs to be renewed in the mind, healed in spirit, and restored in the soul.

> And God called the light Day, and the darkness He called Night. And there was evening and there was morning, one day.
> —Genesis 1:5

> But, beloved, be not ignorant of this one thing, that one day is with the Lord as a thousand years, and a thousand years as one day.
> —2 Peter 3:8

> Having your conversation honest among the Gentiles: that, whereas they speak against you as evildoers, they may by your good works, which they shall behold, glorify God in the day of visitation.
> —1 Peter 2:12

Abraham and Sarah's story gives us the biblical scenario. Sarah, Abraham's wife, was barren, yet God promised Abraham a child with Sarah. When God approached Abraham with the promise of being the father of many nations, Abraham was seventy-five years old. He had been married to Sarah for quite a long time. God had a plan of salvation and restoration for mankind, and it was through Abraham's lineage that the promise would be fulfilled. The earth was already cursed by God because of Adam's disobedience, and God could not go back to the earth to produce another Adam out of the dust of the ground. The new Adam had to come into the earth realm through the womb of a woman who was a chosen vessel unto God. God started this process with Abraham.

There is purpose in everything that God does. God is a holy God, and any vessel He chooses to use must be clean and sanctified for His use. God wanted to use Sarah's womb to incubate a special seed; it was from that seed God was going to produce a breed of people in the earth who would be a holy nation of kings and priests. From the lineage of this seed a child would come who will be Savior and Redeemer, a man named Jesus whose assignment in the earth would be to save people from the power of sin and to destroy the works of the devil.

But Sarah was not a virgin. She had a husband and was not single. To fulfill

His predestined plan for Sarah, God made her womb barren, which prevented her from having children before the season that God designated for His word to her husband, Abraham, to be fulfilled. Also, because they were married, God had to wait until Abraham and Sarah were very, very old, at the state of corruption, in which their bodies were considered dead. A day in the season of life when they had no pleasure or delight in having sexual relations. Abraham and Sarah were practicing abstinence, a complete cessation of sexual activity.

During this period of sexual inactivity, their sexual and reproductive organs and their bodies had gone through the season of purification or sanctification, which is a period of rest called abstinence. But the biblical terminology is Sabbath, from which the word sabbatical is derived. The sabbatical year among the ancient Jews was every seventh year, in which according to the Mosaic Law, the land and vineyards were to remain fallow and debtors were to be released.

God wanted Sarah's firstborn son to be the promise son, and according to the law of the firstborn, he was to be consecrated unto the Lord.

> All the males that first open the womb among your livestock are Mine, whether ox or sheep. But the firstling of a donkey [an unclean beast] you shall redeem with a lamb or kid, and if you do not redeem it, then you shall break its neck. All the firstborn of your sons you shall redeem. And none of you shall appear before Me empty-handed.
> —Exodus 34:19–20

According to the season of life, when a man or a woman's reproductive organs no longer function to produce life, these organs are considered dead. At that state of physical death, Abraham's body could no longer produce the seed of life. At ninety, the monthly periodic custom for women had long ceased to flow for Sarah.

> Now Abraham and Sarah were old, well advanced in years; it had ceased to be with Sarah as with [young] women. [She was past the age of childbearing].
> —Genesis 18:11

> So from one man, though he was physically as good as dead, there have sprung descendants whose number is as the stars of heaven and as countless as the innumerable sands on the seashore.
> —Hebrews 11:12

It was at this state God visited Abraham and Sarah. As Abraham sat in the doorway of his tent, he saw three men coming toward him; one of them was the Lord of Sabaóth, and the other two were angels. Abraham received his guests, and after the hospitality meal the Lord asked for Sarah, and then His word to Abraham was, "I will surely return to you when the season comes round, and behold, Sarah your wife will have a son" (Gen. 18:10).

To understand what transpired in the day of Abraham's visitation by the Lord of Sabaóth, we have to see it in the context that we who were dead in trespasses and sin are born again by the seed of the Word of God. How did Mary, the mother of Jesus, become pregnant with life? The Holy Spirit imparted God's sperm (Word) into Mary when she was unmarried. Mary said, "How can this be seeing that I know not a man?" (Luke 1:34). But Sarah was married; therefore, the seed had to be implanted into her by her husband Abraham. Isaac, the promise seed, was to be a type or symbol of the Christ child who was promised to the world. The natural is always a parallel of the spirit.

When the Lord spoke that word to Abraham, a spiritual transference took place, and Abraham became the receptacle of the life-giving power of God from which Isaac was to be born. When the transference took place, the life-giving power quickened Abraham's dead body and revitalized his dead organs.

> And you [He made alive], when you were dead (slain) by [your] trespasses and sins.
>
> —Ephesians 2:1

> Jesus said to her, I am [Myself] the Resurrection and the Life. Whoever believes in (adheres to, trusts in, and relies on) Me, although he may die, yet he shall live.
>
> —John 11:25

Anyone desiring to marry another spouse after divorce must experience a season of purification and abstinence. Abstinence renders the body dead. This holds true for two single people in a relationship impacted by fornication. There should be a period of celibacy before taking the marriage vows. According to the Mosaic Law, during the sabbatical year, the land and vineyards were to remain fallow, and debtors were to be released.

Fallow is defined as "to remain uncultivated, unused, and unproductive."[3] Fallow land is land that has been plowed but not seeded for one or more growing seasons to kill weeds, to make the soil richer, and to allow the land to rest. It is the plowing of land to be left idle.

Debtor is a person, company, or nation that owes something to another or others.[4]

God's idea for the sabbatical rest included the release of debts. Spiritually, debts are sins we have accumulated that were never purged by the blood of Jesus. The wages of sin or the penalty for sin is death. (See Romans 6:23.) When we partake of the Lord's Sabbath, we consecrate our bodies to the Lord. During this period of consecration we are forgiven of our trespasses as we forgive those who have trespassed against us. As we repent, we experience forgiveness, which is a release of spiritual debts that had us bound to the debtor, Satan.

The idea behind the period of abstinence is for the body to be cleansed from spirits that were transferred into the body during fornication and adultery. During the Old Testament era, God's people and the land of Israel were defiled by idolatry, which is spiritual adultery. God ordered seventy years of captivity for Israel in a strange land, emptying the land of its inhabitants so that the land could keep seventy years of Sabbaths. It was only after seventy years of Sabbath rest that the evil spirits of idolatry were passed out of the land. When Israel returned after the seventy-year captivity, the people of God no longer had a problem with idolatry, and once again the land could be married to Jehovah.

For a spirit to manifest, it needs someone or a body to come into agreement with it. When the people of God were taken into captivity and the land was emptied of its inhabitants, there was no one there to come into agreement with the spirit of idolatry. Therefore, the spirits passed out from the land, seeking habitation elsewhere.

Our body is made of the same substance of the land (earth). If the physical earth that God gave to Israel as an inheritance had to keep the Sabbath to be healed, and for the spirits to pass out of the land, then our body, which is the temple of the Holy Ghost, must abstain from "fleshly lust," which wars against the soul, for our bodies to experience the same type of release and restoration to wholeness. God gave the commandment that we remember the Sabbath day to keep it holy; the Sabbath day is there to remind us on this side of Calvary that there remains a rest unto the people of God.

The duration of the sabbatical rest differs individually and depends on how long the person was involved in adultery and harlotry. For people who have been involved in a promiscuous lifestyle, restoration of the image of God and purification may take some time, but God will give guidance and direction. As a nation, Israel was completely given over to the spirit of harlotry. God's judgment on her was a period of seventy years in captivity or ten seven-year periods of rest for the land while the people were in captivity.

Seven means "complete, finished, rest; fullness, perfection."[5]

Ten means "measure, a period of rest for the measured purpose of accepting or rejecting that which is measured, after a trial or test or temptation; a measure of human responsibility."[6]

For a person to remarry after divorce the accepted sabbatical rest is one year. A person who has had multiple sexual partners or a lifestyle of prostitution and infidelity, which is classified as sins against the body, the healing process may take longer. A period of deliverance, rebuilding, realignment, restoration, and consecration must first take place for the evil spirits to be purged out of the body.

There are women and men who were driven into a lifestyle of promiscuity because of other issues, such as repeated molestation, rape, and incest. If they are single, they need abstinence along with therapy to rebuild their self-esteem. Anyone who has been involved in hard-core sexual sins, like pornography, prostitution, and sodomy, must go to a greater spiritual depth in their relationship with God, in comparison to the depth of sin from which they were delivered, to overcome and conquer the demons that had them bound, because temptations will always be present.

Men who have had their physical features altered because of demonic sexual activity, and have experienced the misalignment of the soul, the seat of their personality, must go through a sabbatical rest for deliverance, realignment, and restoration so that the image of God in them can be restored. Satan has assignments on the lives of people who came out of hard sin, and the slayer of destiny would always be pursuing them, watching and waiting for the opportunity to put them back into bondage.

> But when the unclean spirit has gone out of a man, it roams through dry [arid] places in search of rest, but it does not find any.
>
> Then it says, I will go back to my house from which I came out. And when it arrives, it finds the place unoccupied, swept, put in order, and decorated.
>
> Then it goes and brings with it seven other spirits more wicked than itself, and they go in and make their home there. And the last

condition of that man becomes worse than the first. So also shall it be with this wicked generation.

—Matthew 12:43–45

When a sexual stronghold or soul tie is broken in one's life, the soul will feel the release. Because the soul is the seat of our emotions, when that break-through comes, many people react with uncontrollable crying because the bondage is broken off and the soul is now free.

Healing and deliverance depends on a person's commitment to Christ. Some people develop and put on Christ faster than others because they put more into their spiritual growth and development. But along with purification by abstinence, reading the Word, fasting, and prayer, a person may have to go through the physical act of deliverance for a demon to be cast out that refuses to leave on its own accord.

The Book of Esther tells us that the women who were qualified to spend a night with the king had to go through twelve months of purification and abstinence.

> Now when the turn of each maiden came to go in to King Ahasuerus, after the regulations for the women had been carried out for twelve months—since this was the regular period for their beauty treatments, six months with oil of myrrh and six months with sweet spices and perfumes and the things for the purifying of the women.
>
> —Esther 2:12

There was no way a woman could go from another man's bed to the king's bed without purification. Furthermore, to avoid that problem, the king's servants put out the call for single, young virgins only. That was the qualifying factor that enabled a young maiden to be considered and to be eligible to become queen.

Preparation for Marriage After Divorce

Preparation denotes the act or process of preparing, the condition of being prepared, readiness, something done to prepare, and something prepared for a special occasion.[7]

We are assuming that every marriage that ends in divorce is a bad experience that has affected either one or both parties negatively. Some have said it is the best decision they have ever made because of the mental and spiritual condition of the person they were married to.

Breaking soul ties

Divorce is the death of a marriage or the termination of a covenant relationship. The impact of divorce is felt in the soul of individuals who have been married for some time or have truly loved their spouse. Divorce affects the soul (the mind, will, emotions, and intellect), and in many cases it causes financial hardship to the abandoned family. Even though divorce gives one a legal separation on paper, when two have become *one* through sexual intimacy and covenant, any tearing apart causes damage to the emotions. We love with our emotions, and the deeper the affection and desire for the spouse, the harder it is for the soul to be unraveled or untangled from the bond of intimacy. The damage in some cases can be irreparable without therapy and inner healing.

The soul can be bound up by the trauma it has experienced for many, many years. The power of the soul must be understood, because a defect in the soul causes hurt and wounded people to retaliate or react with negativity. Some of the symptoms of a broken soul are unforgiveness, hate, anger, murder, strife, confusion, rejection, sadness, low self-esteem, pride, conceitedness, critical behavior, competitive jealousy, the need for attention, lack of boundaries, the need for affirmation and validation, identity crises, bitterness, envy, pretending to be something they are not, sabotage, depression, self-pity, and other emotions.

A soul tie is passion that cannot subside (whether it is love or hate) long after a relationship has disintegrated. That passion tells you that there is still an attachment that cannot be broken by the will of a person. A soul tie is bondage to another person or thing that can only be loosed by that person identifying and acknowledging the problem and seeking God for deliverance. People with soul ties continue to love or hate the betrayer who rejected them for years after they both have moved on with their lives. The spirit of their soul mate remains with them and possesses them as long as they maintain their passion, desire, or hate for their ex-lover. Some soul ties are rooted in unforgiveness, low self-esteem, rejection, etc. Many people with soul ties develop sicknesses, diseases, depression, bitterness, a retaliatory personality, and continue to suffer emotionally for years and eventually die from a broken heart.

Even if a person with a soul tie remarries, emotionally their soul is still caught in the grip of entanglement with their former spouse. These second marriages seldom last because of the underlying issues and the baggage that was brought into the second marriage. There must be a sabbatical period of rest and deliverance for the soul to be restored. When people with unresolved issues try to replace an offending spouse with another, that relationship does not last because the second marriage is not built on a strong foundation of love and trust. Where there is emotion and passion, whether good or bad for the offending partner, his or her spirit will continue to dominate all their relationships.

One of my assignments is to minister to women. Our ministry, Woman to Woman, is designed to deal with women in the body of Christ who are called of God but don't understand proper boundaries and protocol in ministry and relationships. We identify and validate the call of God in their life and assist them in getting to know who they are by separating the issues from their divine purpose. We also help them to understand how behavior that stems from a place of brokenness and unforgiveness can hinder their walk with God and their ability to minister the love of God to others.

Soul ties must be broken. If not, there will be no true harmony or genuine love. No matter how hard the new spouse tries, all their efforts will be rewarded with criticisms and contradictions. And, if the new partner does not understand the dynamics of the soul, they will give up out of frustration and regret.

Here are some things to consider before remarrying:

- Wounds of the heart
- Unforgiveness
- Habits
- Lusts of the flesh
- Lust of the eye
- Pride of life
- Jealousy
- Unfaithfulness
- Godliness
- Is this person really in love with you?
- Does this person want to remarry on the rebound?
- Is this person responsible and accountable with their finance?

- What kind of relationship do they have with family members?

- Do they have a spirit of retaliation?

- Do they have a spirit of anger?

- Do they enjoy sexual perversion?

- Is this person possessive and selfish?

- Is this person controlling and manipulative?

- Do they have a lazy disposition?

- Am I dealing with a liar?

Another very important fact to consider is that many people who have lived alone for quite some time become set in their ways and do not want to change or compromise to accommodate a new spouse. They have a soul tie with their independence. If a person is considering marriage after divorce, they must first reject the spirit of divorce and pray to know God's perfect will for their life.

Here are some tips for praying the will of God before remarrying:

- Pray for God's will, and ask Him to lead you to the partner He has chosen for you.

- Pray that God would give you wisdom.

- Pray that His Word will be the root and foundation of the relationship.

- Pray for your total healing and deliverance from the bad impact of past relationships.

- Pray that God would show you his or her heart.

- Pray that God would not let you fall under the influence of the spirit of manipulation, confusion, and control.

- Plead the blood of Jesus against any satanic attachments or assignments in the name of Jesus.

- Bind the activities of the spirit of flirtation, infatuation, strange women and strange men, lust, ungodly attachment to the wrong choice of a spouse, spiritual blindness and deafness, spirit wives or spirit husbands.

- Break and renounce all soul ties, and plead the blood of Jesus to wash them all away.

- Loose yourself from all evil affections, emotions, and desires, and submit your soul, body, and spirit to the Holy Spirit.

- Release yourself from mind control, and break every marital curse in the name of Jesus.

- Bind the spirit of marriage destruction in the name of Jesus.

- Command every demonic in-law to loose their grip and release their hold on you and your spouse in the name of Jesus.

- Ask the Lord to send out His angels to the east, west, north, and south to bring your provisions, blessings, and goods needed for a successful marriage in the name of Jesus. Amen.

Premarital counseling

There are reasons why premarital counseling is very important. One reason is that it gives the couple a platform to express their views and state what their expectations are. This provides opportunity to discover any hidden agendas. It allows them to know their spouse's predispositions on each other's role in the relationship, how they are going to relate to in-laws, and how their finances are going to be handled. It will also determine what are the strengths and weaknesses of each spouse and what each can contribute mentally, morally, spiritually, and financially to the union.

As Christians, we are free to marry in the Lord. Premarital counseling will help to answer pertinent questions the couple has not considered, especially if the union is a blending of cultures.

What should a person do if he or she has discovered that their intended spouse has a criminal record or is wanted by the police in another state for a heinous crime? Or what should they do if they discover that their intended mate had a spouse that died under suspicious circumstances. Or the man has children that he never claimed to avoid child support? Or he is still in love with his first wife, or the woman is still in love with her first husband? When the intended spouse has too much debt, with no way to have it paid off, and has bad credit, how will this affect their ability to purchase a home? What if the intended spouse is irresponsible with finances—who will carry the burden of the mortgage? Premarital counseling should expose these hidden issues.

The human heart is so deceptive that many things may not come out in counseling, but there is a God in heaven who reveals secrets. If we let Him be our guide in all that we do, we will avoid many of the pitfalls and snares of the enemy. Women especially must be wise enough to look beyond the outward pretense and flattery to really know the spirit and character of the individual.

Premarital counseling will help the couple to understand if they are ready to give up their singleness and to be part of a union, or if they should wait until they are a bit more mature, especially if they desire to marry into a cross-cultural relationship. The counselor should determine the duration of the period for counseling before the marriage. If there was prior sexual battery, physical abuse, or drug addiction, problems can arise after the fact, and the intended spouse must know these facts.

Juanita (not her real name) became promiscuous because she was sexually abused by her father continually until she left home. By then she was eighteen and pregnant. She was marked for life, even though she had escaped from the clutches of her father. Juanita needed professional help and had to go through extensive therapy for her healing before she could marry. A broken woman cannot function as a whole person. If she is married to a man who is ignorant of the effects of sexual abuse, he would be incapable of assisting her if his mind is only on his sexual needs being met. His understanding and support is vital to her recovery.

Also, many young men are void of direction because their father abandoned the family, abused their mother, and did not provide for a stable home environment for the family. How are they going to be good fathers if they never had a pattern of a good father to emulate? These issues need to be addressed in premarital counseling, where the man should be able to express to his intended spouse how growing up without a father has affected his life.

In premarital counseling a couple should set boundaries and limits for in-laws, friends, and relations. Mothers-in-law and sisters-in-law who are controlling and out of order must have stated boundaries and limits, especially if they have no husbands and perceive their brother or son as their property to control and counsel at their will.

But most of all, prayer must be a vital part of a Christian home and must be included in family time. Praying together, blessing each other, and keeping Christ at the center of family life and relationships will keep all antimarriage forces away and out of the home.

In Christian marriages the father's blessing is important. If there is no father available, the pastor's blessing will supersede the father's blessing.

Chapter 7

COMMUNICATION

But to do good and to communicate forget not.
—HEBREWS 13:16, KJV

CIENTISTS HAVE DISCOVERED THAT THE MALE BRAIN IS DIFFERENT from the female brain. During fetal development, around the sixteenth week in the mother's womb, when the male organs are positioning, the chromosomes in his brain also change, affecting the communication links between the right and left hemispheres of the brain. Now he no longer has the same ability to communicate freely his feelings as females do, who have both sides of their brain easily accessible. Thus, the male becomes more logical in his approach to life. It is not that he doesn't have emotions, but because of the reduced chromosome link between the left and right hemisphere of his brain, he isn't as easily in touch with them, nor can he easily communicate his feelings. This fact alone brings major problems in a marriage if this fact is not understood.

The most important part of communication is listening. Listening is verbal and nonverbal communication. To listen means to make a conscious effort to hear, so as to give heed. It also means to pay attention to or to take advice or instructions. As a teacher, Jesus would often end His teachings by saying, "He who has ears to hear, let him hear" (Matt. 11:15, NKJV).

Communication is vital in relationships, not only with our spouses but also in every aspect of life. Without communication, there will be misunderstanding and chaos. Goals will be unattainable without communication because human beings are interdependent on each another for resources and information. The Creator of the universe is a communicator. The first words we have recorded that He spoke were, "Let there be light," but before the foundation of the world, before time existed, He was communicating His thoughts. His first recorded words were an expression of those thoughts.

During His ministry on Earth, Jesus taught His disciples many lessons by parables. There was a message of redemption in each parable. The crowds heard the parables but did not understand the message, but He gave the understanding of the message to His disciples. It was very important that His disciples heard His words and received them within their spirit, because through His words He was revealing to them the mysteries of the kingdom and imparting not only understanding and the wisdom of the kingdom but also life. The only way they could receive His life was by hearing His words.

His Word lets us know that before man came into existence, God had a plan of redemption for mankind. His Word implies that before the existence of time, God determined that His Son, whom we know as Jesus, was going to be the sacrificial lamb that would die for the sins of the world and, in so doing, would satisfy God's demands for justice for man's rebellion against Him. Therefore, there had to be a consensus of agreement in the Godhead when God spoke before time, and it was agreed upon, written, and ratified in the counsels of the heavens that His Son would come to the earth as Savior, and in this capacity, He would be required to taste death for every man. This, according to the predetermined counsel of God, would come into manifestation in the fullness of time and would be God's way of communicating His love to mankind.

> For God so loved the world that He gave His only begotten Son, that whoever believes in Him should not perish but have everlasting life.
> —John 3:16, NKJV

It is said that the soul is the seat of our personality, and everything we have experienced in life, whether pleasure or pain, has left an indelible mark on our soul. From our early childhood, the home environment, school environment, our relationship with our parents and siblings, the traumas and the joys of life, every experience good or bad, has left its mark on our soul and has been the impetus that has shaped our personality, our responses, our behavior, and has affected the way we love or hate and communicate.

Personality is a combination of many factors. Personality identifies the individuality of a person by (a) habitual patterns and qualities of behavior, (b) by distinctive physical, mental activities, attitudes, and qualities of the person, (c) personal attractiveness, and (d) offensive or disparaging nature or disposition.

Each of us has a different personality type and certain levels of comfort or discomfort in the way we express ourselves and communicate with others.

What is the most common complaint that women have about their husbands? They do not listen. What is the most common complaint husbands have about their wives? She fusses too much. Well, women fuss because men do not listen, and men don't listen because women fuss.

How do we resolve conflicts in relationships? One way is to listen to the heart of the other partner; another way is to engage in communication and healthy discussions with the right attitude. Attitude is an indicator that expresses disposition, mood, and the state of the mind or feeling with regard to some matter. A hostile attitude never facilitates resolution, but a soft answer with a conciliatory attitude diffuses anger.

Writing personal letters to each other is still an effective form of communication because it gives one the opportunity to express oneself and explain actions that were misunderstood. This is where our individual personalities play a pivotal part in relationships. We don't always have to agree but we can refrain from being disagreeable.

If we are afraid to confront, ask the right questions, and settle our differences in the fear of God, there will always be that undermining spirit of suspicion that would cause strife and dissention in the ranks. Women or men who are intimidated by a strong-willed partner will not identify a problem and call it out because they are afraid of confrontation.

Godly parents are to be role models for their children, and one way of teaching and training the next generation is by example. Yelling and screaming at each other is an ineffective way of communication; one partner may use this method to gain control, but this form of communication sends the wrong message to the next generation. This method of communication is employed by people who are unable to control their environment except by intimidation. If one partner submits to intimidation to maintain peace in the relationship, the silent partner will have unresolved issues in their heart, which will affect communication.

Misunderstanding is caused by preconceived notions and assumptions about people or about a situation. Misunderstanding also occurs when we do not have the correct information or prior knowledge so that we can make an informed decision. When we assume and pass judgment on people and their motives without just cause, it causes misunderstanding. It is easy to misunderstand a person if they speak a different language, if they did not share their thoughts or personal information, or if they are from a different culture. If we use assumptions when we are uninformed, we will be guilty of stereotyping, and we will react to people who are different in a negative way.

The kingdom of God is countercultural to the culture of any region, nation, or country. The kingdom of God is often opposed by the demonic strongholds in any community of people who resist God's truth, but God has various means of expressing and relating truth to people. In the Old Testament He spoke through prophets, angels, dreams, visions, symbolic types, signs, and wonders. In the New Testament God communicates through His Word.

Communication has various forms of verbal and nonverbal expressions, which we call language. Language is any method of communicating ideas by a system of signs, symbols, gestures, or the like. It is also the transmission of meaning, feeling, or intent by corresponding action. Language involves the use of vocal sounds in meaningful patterns, and the corresponding written symbols to form, express, and communicate thoughts and feelings. All created beings have some form of sound that is their language and their means of communication.

THE POWER OF WORDS

The spoken word or the written word is the most powerful form of expression and communication between God and man. Words are a combination of sounds, or its representation in writing or printing that symbolizes and communicates a meaning. It is something that is said, a remark, comment, an utterance, a discourse, a command, an order, direction, a dispute, argument, conversation, or a statement.

In Creation, God used the power of words to form the universe. All creation, the world, and all of nature came into manifestation through the power of words.

> [But] in the last of these days He has spoken to us in [the person of a] Son, Whom He appointed Heir and lawful Owner of all things, also by and through Whom He created the worlds and the reaches of space and the ages of time [He made, produced, built, operated, and arranged them in order].
>
> He is the sole expression of the glory of God [the Light-being, the out-raying or radiance of the divine], and He is the perfect imprint and very image of [God's] nature, upholding and maintaining and guiding and propelling the universe by His mighty word of power.

When He had by offering Himself accomplished our cleansing of sins and riddance of guilt, He sat down at the right hand of the divine Majesty on high.

—Hebrews 1:2–3

Man, who was created in the image and likeness of God, was given the same ability and authority to use words to create a positive or negative environment. We speak life or death with words. If there is a negative, hostile atmosphere in our homes, someone created that environment with the power of words.

With words we pray; bless our family; instruct; correct; transact business; express our love and devotion; communicate our thoughts, ideas, and emotions; worship God; and give thanks. Without the ability to verbally express ourselves or to create sound, the world would be a very silent place.

In politics and government, words can have a positive or a negative impact on a candidate's bid for election. Nations have gone to war over words that incited riot. Civil wars among tribes have continued for decades because of offensive language used by opposing fractions. Words have the power to alter the course or direction of a person's life. Verbal abuse has been cited as the cause of many marriages going on the rocks and eventually dissolving. Words are so important that Jesus said, "But I say unto you, That every idle word that men shall speak, they shall give account thereof in the day of judgment" (Matt. 12:36, kjv).

If one's spouse is an unbeliever, the sanctified spouse can decree and declare the blessing of salvation upon the unbelieving spouse. If we refrain from negativity in the home, the power of positive words can be used to impart, activate, and stir up the gifts of God in our children. When we make a habit of speaking life over our spouse and giving a positive prophetic response to the challenges of the powers of darkness, the effect of peace will be righteousness. This would not be easy if our flesh is not disciplined. We cannot pray and speak positive confessions then speak negatively when we are angry. The negative cancels out the positive. Many relationships have fallen by the wayside because of negative words. Relationships between friends and other family members have been ruined forever because of negative words or evil degrees. But Jesus gave the antidote for the spirit of slander, gossip, propaganda, lying, character assassination, and evil degrees by in-laws and outlaws.

But I tell you, love your enemies and pray for those who persecute you.

—Matthew 5:44

God hates falsehood, which is a biblical word for lies. Anyone who concocts a story, and the one who repeats and spreads vicious and false rumors based upon that story, becomes a liar. A liar is a slanderer, and a talebearer is a liar. Satan is the father of lies; the truth is not in him. Jesus said, "He is a liar, and the father of it" (John 8:44, KJV).

> Let no corrupt communication proceed out of your mouth, but that which is good to the use of edifying, that it may minister grace unto the hearers.
>
> —Ephesians 4:29, KJV

> Put away from you false and dishonest speech, and willful and contrary talk put far from you.
>
> —Proverbs 4:24

DISCIPLINE IS A METHOD OF COMMUNICATION

> And the Lord said, Shall I hide from Abraham [My friend and servant] what I am going to do, since Abraham shall surely become a great and mighty nation, and all the nations of the earth shall be blessed through him and shall bless themselves by him?
> For I have known (chosen, acknowledged) him [as My own], so that he may teach and command his children and the sons of his house after him to keep the way of the Lord and to do what is just and righteous, so that the Lord may bring Abraham what He has promised him.
>
> —Genesis 18:17–19

God acknowledged the fact that He knew the kind of man Abraham was, a man that was going to discipline his household to keep the way of the Lord, which is a righteous man's responsibility as the head of the household.

Children need instructions, correction, and training that will develop their individual gifts and teach them self-control, orderly conduct, and submission to authority, all of which would produce good character. Where there is a lack of discipline, there will be a lack of boundaries, uncontrollable behavior, no self-control, and eventually bad character. Children need a system of rules that will govern their conduct. It does not matter how gifted or intelligent a child is; if they have never been disciplined, they will become a problem to themselves and eventually to society.

Government on a state and federal level has had to enact legislation whereby the judicial system can order disciplinary action for undisciplined children who became undisciplined adults. Society has to pick up the tab for the mistakes made in the home. Discipline is the responsibility of the parents, whether it is a one or two-parent household. When there is no order and stability in the parents' relationship, children very often go undisciplined.

It is said that young men are closer to their mothers than to their fathers. In the early years, all mothers nurture, cuddle, and bond with their kids, but there are instances, especially when the father in not in the home or involved in the life of his son, that certain mothers go to the extreme to be the father and the mother to her son and will continue to nurture, cuddle, and spoil him way beyond the period of adolescence and maturity. Some will continue to live at home well into their adulthood. This causes some sons to be emotionally and financially dependent on their mothers. When he leaves his mother's house to live with his wife, he brings all his dependency and dysfunction into that relationship, and his wife is stuck with a boy pretending to be a man, who wants all his toys and no responsibility.

Most undisciplined children become demanding, assertive, rebellious, and out of control. At the age when boys are transitioning into manhood, a stronger authoritative voice is needed for that level of maturity. Many women will continue to give in to the demands of their grown sons well into their age of accountability. By doing so she is sending a message to her son that will affect the way he relates to and communicates with women he has relationships with. My own mother, who was a blessed Christian woman, never worked outside of the home. She, along with the women of her generation, subscribed to the belief that sons did not have to do any chores around the house because housework was woman's work. That mind-set produced a generation of men that are messy and untidy.

Out of that old mind-set has emerged a new generation of women who are educated business leaders and business owners and women who are financially independent, who own their own homes, drive their own cars, and pay their own bills. They are not dependent on a man for anything but love and respect within the confines of a committed relationship. They expect their husbands to do chores around the house and to help with the responsibility of raising the children. That theory about men not doing chores around the home is outdated and passed away with the lifestyle of the previous generation. Unless a family of two working parents can afford to hire someone to clean the house and take out the trash, every member of the family must share in the responsibility of keeping the home clean and in proper order.

Husbands and wives must be examples to their children. That is the first step in discipline. In my use of the term *discipline*, my primary emphasis is on teaching that motivates and causes to mature. Discipline is the assessment of behavioral guidelines. It is the explanation of behavioral expectations to the end that the one disciplined is enabled to understand both what is expected and why it is expected.

Discipline goes beyond demands and intimidation. Its purpose is not only to achieve right behavior, but also to progressively lessen dependence upon the disciplinary authority. External discipline that fails to result in self-discipline fails altogether. Though we as parents expect children to obey us without question, we must acknowledge that questions will arise as a child grows. Discipline should answer these questions.

Discipline, properly conceived, is an instructional task. It is inclusive of virtually all teaching efforts, whether employed in group or personal settings. The punitive dimension of discipline is our second consideration. Punishment is that which is brought to bear when behavioral guidelines have been transgressed. It is the penalty for failure to do right when right is known. Punishment must follow instruction or it is out of order.

Good discipline also includes mention of sure consequences of misconduct. Punishment is administered when discipline is not heeded. It is unjust and potentially damaging to the relationship to punish a child who does not know his action is wrong, why it is wrong, or what the consequences of his action will be.

The goal of discipline is to develop the mind and spirit. It molds and strengthens character, produces an awareness of righteousness, and builds sufficient inner strength to do right when right is known.

Discipline is a developmental task, a progressive exercise. The more one's own character is developed, the less dependent that person is on external authority.

CULTURE, CUSTOMS, AND TRADITIONS

So for the sake of your tradition (the rules handed down by your forefathers), you have set aside the Word of God [depriving it of force and authority and making it of no effect].

—MATTHEW 15:6

In this world there is a lot of movement as prophesied by Daniel the prophet. (See Daniel 12:4.) People are moving to and fro in the earth, migrating and settling in different parts of the world away from their land of origin. In major cities around the world there is always a dominant culture, yet one can see major differences in ethnicity, language, and religion among the inhabitants.

The kingdom of God is a melting pot of culture, customs, traditions, and people of all nations who have accepted Jesus Christ as Lord and Savior. What is common to all citizens of the kingdom is the Word of God, the Spirit of Christ, and the blood of Jesus. We are a kingdom of priests and kings, a chosen generation, a royal priesthood, a holy nation, and a peculiar people. We are also known as the generation of Jesus Christ, sons of God, and we are joint heirs with Jesus. We have a spiritual culture and a language, part of which is prayer, the Pentecost experience, the language of the Holy Spirit, worship to our God and King, and a lifestyle based on our rule of faith, doctrine, and the commandments of God.

There will always be interracial and intercultural marriages among men, including the body of Christ. But wisdom dictates that if one marries outside of their natural ethnicity and culture, they must understand that there are differences they will have to embrace, and adjustments will have to be made for there to be understanding and cohesiveness in the relationship.

To try to change your spouse to be more like you would be foolish. I once saw a couple at an airport. The woman was a German Caucasian who was engaged to a black, Caribbean man, and they were on their way to meet his parents. She was dressed with a black Afro wig and an African-style outfit. She was pretending to be black to impress his family, but her outlandish outfit and wig caught the attention of everyone in the airport. People were just staring at her because she looked out of place, like a masquerade. She wanted to identify with another culture so she could be accepted. However, if her fiancé was looking for a black woman to marry, there were many available, but he chose her because he loved her, and all she needed to do was to be her natural-born self and let his family accept her for who she was, a German Caucasian woman.

The kingdom of God is global, and as the sons of God, we must accept diversity. Diversity is a kingdom requisite. Each nation and its people have its own distinctiveness other than language. There are differences in culinary skills, music, clothing, and the generational belief system and practice that define culture, morals, and tradition.

When a person moves away from his or her homeland and takes up residence in another country, they take certain identifying marks with them. One of these identifying marks is their religious belief and practice. Religion is part of the culture of some families, and this must be taken into consideration before marriage. Nations have gone to war over religion. I believe that if a person's faith means that much to them, then they should marry someone of the same faith. However, religion does not constitute relationship with God. In premarital counseling, religion should be discussed before the couples take their marriage vow. To assume that a person wants any part of their spouse's religion is presumptuous. Men or women have pursued someone who is the object of their affection into the church and continued to attend faithfully to please their spouse, but remained an unchanged unbeliever and skeptic, who did not want a relationship with Jesus Christ.

Another point we must take into consideration is this: A spouse should not have to abandon his or her culture or language because they fell in love with someone of a different nationality. A common language should be spoken in the home, but the children from that union should embrace both cultures and languages. Religious persuasions and affiliations can be changed if a spouse is willing to make the adjustment. But this question must be asked: Can two walk together if they are not in agreement?

RUTH AND NAOMI

There was a famine in Israel in the days of the Judges, which caused the migration of an Israelite man with his wife (Naomi) and their two sons to the country of Moab. Shortly after the marriage of their sons to two Moabite women, the three men in the family died.

Naomi decided to go back to her homeland and insisted that her two daughters-in-law return to the home of their parents. But her daughter-in-law Ruth insisted on staying with her mother-in-law. When Naomi saw the determination in Ruth to follow her, she said no more, and they both arrived at Bethlehem in the land of Israel.

> And Ruth said, Urge me not to leave you or to turn back from following you; for where you go I will go, and where you lodge I will lodge. Your people shall be my people and your God my God.
> Where you die I will die, and there will I be buried. The Lord do so to me, and more also, if anything but death parts me from you.
> —RUTH 1:16–17

Ruth embraced not only her mother-in-law, but she also embraced her culture, tradition, and religion. She lived with her mother-in-law and provided for the older woman. According to the custom and tradition in Israel, when a man died without seed, the younger brother or next of kin had to marry his widow and raise up seed for the older brother so that his name would not be blotted out in the ancestral line of Israel. The younger brother inherited his wife and the land, which was a part of the father's inheritance to sons.

As an older woman, Naomi was not able to give birth to any more children, so she encouraged her two daughters-in-law to go away and find husbands among their own people. But Ruth cleaved to her mother-in-law and followed her back to her country, and they arrived in Bethlehem at the time of Barley harvest.

In Bethlehem there was a man who was next of kin to Elimelech, Naomi's deceased husband. He, according to the ancestral line was in second place to purchase the inheritance of Naomi's husband. But along with the inheritance, the redeemer kinsman had to marry Naomi's daughter-in-law, who was a Moabite. The kinsman, who was first in line forfeited his right of redemption, allowing Boaz to redeem the inheritance and take Ruth, the Moabites, as his wife.

Ruth said to Naomi, "Let me go now to the field and glean," because strangers, widows, and the poor were at liberty to glean behind the reapers. It was a privilege granted or refused according to the good will or the favor of the owner. But Ruth, according to divine providence, came to the field belonging to Boaz. He was an older man, but he was related to Naomi's husband. Ruth found favor with Boaz because he had heard of all the kindness she had done for her mother-in-law since the death of her husband.

On hearing that Ruth had gleaned in the field of Boaz, the older woman asked Ruth's permission to seek a home and rest for her that she might prosper in the land and among the people that she came to embrace. With Ruth's consent, she began to advise her to wash and anoint herself, to put on her best clothes and go down to the threshing floor. Naomi also advised her not to let the man know she was there until he was finished eating and drinking. She was to watch for the place where he would lie down for the night, and after he fell asleep, she would go quietly and lie at his feet and pull his covers over herself.

Ruth was obedient. Naomi knew the customs and traditions of her people, and Ruth did not. The act of lying at Boaz's feet symbolized that she was acknowledging his duty as a kinsman. There was no impropriety in the action, just a reminder to Boaz of the duty that was expected of him as the kinsman of her deceased husband. It would have been out of order for Naomi or Ruth to take control of the situation by telling Boaz what he should or should not do.

Lying crosswise at his feet was a position that Eastern servants frequently took when they slept in the same chamber or tent with their master. If they wanted a covering, custom allowed them that benefit from part of the covering on their master's bed, to spread the skirt over them as symbolic action denoting protection.

In cultures of the East, if anyone puts his skirt over a woman, it is synonymous with saying that he is married to her. At all marriages of the modern Jews and the Hindu religion, one part of the ceremony is for the bridegroom to put a silken or cotton cloak around his bride.

> And he [Boaz] said, Who art thou? And she answered, I am Ruth thine handmaid: spread therefore thy skirt over thine handmaid; for thou art a near kinsman.
>
> —RUTH 3:9, KJV

Ruth made a good impression on this man great of wealth and distinction among his people. She was a woman who adopted the culture and tradition of another nation, and she submitted to the mentorship of her mother-in-law and followed through with the instructions she was given. According to custom, Naomi knew that after Boaz had given his word to Ruth, all she had to do was sit still and wait.

Boaz then went up to the city's gate and met with the elders and the first next of kin. Since Ruth had embraced his religion and his people, now Boaz, in a public manner and before the elders of his people, became her redeemer kinsman and married Ruth. She conceived a son, and Naomi became the son's nurse. And the women said to Naomi:

> And the women said unto Naomi, Blessed be the LORD, which hath not left thee this day without a kinsman, that his name may be famous in Israel. And he shall be unto thee a restorer of thy life, and a nourisher of thine old age: for thy daughter in law, which loveth thee, which is better to thee than seven sons, hath born him.
>
> —RUTH 4:14–15, KJV

Chapter 8

GOD'S DISSERTATION ON MARRIAGE

When the foundations are being destroyed, what can the righteous do?

—Psalm 11:3, niv

GOD IS THE SAME YESTERDAY, TODAY, AND FOREVER. GOD HAS NOT changed His position on marriage. His original thought, plan, and design for marriage remains the same. He is a Father, who in His wisdom and foresight created an institution called marriage for the procreation and preservation of the seed of His children.

Satan is persistent in his warfare against women because the seed of life is incubated in her womb for a gestational period of time before it is released in the earth. All of nature and the kingdom of God exist and promulgate itself by the seed principle. The principle of life is in the seed that the woman carries. It is through this seed that life is perpetuated in the earth to bring forth a new generation after the old generation passes through the doorway of death.

Satan is a murderer who hates life; he cannot give birth to anything because he is a malignant, destructive entity who has death, destruction, lies, and stealing embedded in his DNA. Each time a soul is destroyed with death, God releases fresh seed in the earth through the womb of the woman. Women keep the cycle of life continuing in the earth. Every entity that has come into the earth realm had to enter through a womb. Satan and his demonic hordes are the only entities that operate in the earth without coming through the legal doorway of the womb. Therefore, Satan cannot produce life; he can only destroy life, and because of this his warfare against marriage, the seed of the woman, and the headship of man is relentless.

The woman was taken out of the man, but out of the woman comes forth the man. She gives birth to life, a new generation, new hopes, new possibilities, and dreams. Satan's weapon of choice is death. The seed of the woman is his object of jealousy and hate. It is through the seed of the woman that the Redeemer, the Christ child, came into the earth; it is through the seed of the woman many preachers of the gospel have been released in the earth; it is through the seed of the woman that the church, the bride of Christ, will one day rule and reign with Christ in His glorious kingdom.

God rebuked Israel for the way husbands were offending their wives, by abusing them like the heathen nations around them.

> And this you do with double guilt; you cover the altar of the Lord with tears [shed by your unoffending wives, divorced by you that you might take heathen wives], and with [your own] weeping and crying out because the Lord does not regard your offering any more or accept it with favor at your hand.
>
> Yet you ask, Why does He reject it? Because the Lord was witness [to the covenant made at your marriage] between you and the wife of your youth, against whom you have dealt treacherously and to whom you were faithless. Yet she is your companion and the wife of your covenant [made by your marriage vows].
>
> And did not God make [you and your wife] one [flesh]? Did not One make you and preserve your spirit alive? And why [did God make you two] one? Because He sought a godly offspring [from your union]. Therefore take heed to yourselves, and let no one deal treacherously and be faithless to the wife of his youth.
>
> For the Lord, the God of Israel, says: I hate divorce and marital separation and him who covers his garment [his wife] with violence. Therefore keep a watch upon your spirit [that it may be controlled by My Spirit], that you deal not treacherously and faithlessly [with your marriage mate].
>
> You have wearied the Lord with your words. Yet you say, In what way have we wearied Him? [You do it when by your actions] you say, Everyone who does evil is good in the sight of the Lord and He delights in them. Or [by asking], Where is the God of justice?
>
> —MALACHI 2:13–17

THE APOSTLE PAUL'S ADMONITION ON MARRIAGE

Be subject to one another out of reverence for Christ (the Messiah, the Anointed One). Wives, be subject (be submissive and adapt yourselves) to your own husbands as [a service] to the Lord. For the husband is head of the wife as Christ is the Head of the church, Himself the Savior of [His] body. As the church is subject to Christ, so let wives also be subject in everything to their husbands. Husbands, love your wives, as Christ loved the church and gave Himself up for her, So that He might sanctify her, having cleansed her by the washing of water with the Word, That He might present the church to Himself in glorious splendor, without spot or wrinkle or any such things [that she might be holy and faultless]. Even so husbands should love their wives as [being in a sense] their own bodies. He who loves his own wife loves himself. For no man ever hated his own flesh, but nourishes and carefully protects and cherishes it, as Christ does the church, Because we are members (parts) of His body. For this reason a man shall leave his father and his mother and shall be joined to his wife, and the two shall become one flesh. This mystery is very great, but I speak concerning [the relation of] Christ and the church. However, let each man of you [without exception] love his wife as [being in a sense] his very own self; and let the wife see that she respects and reverences her husband [that she notices him, regards him, honors him, prefers him, venerates, and esteems him; and that she defers to him, praises him, and loves and admires him exceedingly].

—EPHESIANS 5:21–33

THE APOSTLE PETER'S DISCOURSE ON MARRIAGE

Wives, in the same way be submissive to your husbands so that, if any of them do not believe the word, they may be won over without words by the behavior of their wives, when they see the purity and reverence of your lives. Your beauty should not come from outward adornment, such as braided hair and the wearing of gold jewelry and fine clothes. Instead, it should be that of your inner self, the unfading beauty of a gentle and quiet spirit, which is of great worth in God's sight. For this is the way the holy women of the past who put their hope in God used to make themselves beautiful. They were submissive to their own husbands, like Sarah, who obeyed Abraham and called him her master. You are her daughters if you do what is right and do not give way to fear.

Husbands, in the same way be considerate as you live with your wives, and treat them with respect as the weaker partner and as heirs with you of the gracious gift of life, so that nothing will hinder your prayers.

Finally, all of you, live in harmony with one another; be sympathetic, love as brothers, be compassionate and humble. Do not repay evil with evil or insult with insult, but with blessing, because to this you were called so that you may inherit a blessing. For, "Whoever would love life and see good days must keep his tongue from evil and his lips from deceitful speech. He must turn from evil and do good; he must seek peace and pursue it. For the eyes of the Lord are on the righteous and his ears are attentive to their prayer, but the face of the Lord is against those who do evil."

—1 PETER 3:1–12, NIV

JESUS' TEACHINGS ON MARRIAGE

You have heard that it was said, You shall not commit adultery. But I say to you that everyone who so much as looks at a woman with evil desire for her has already committed adultery with her in his heart.

—MATTHEW 5:27–28

It has also been said, Whoever divorces his wife must give her a certificate of divorce. But I tell you, Whoever dismisses and repudiates and divorces his wife, except on the grounds of unfaithfulness (sexual immorality), causes her to commit adultery, and whoever marries a woman who has been divorced commits adultery.

—MATTHEW 5:31–32

Appendix A

APOSTOLIC DECLARATIONS FOR YOUR MARRIAGE

- I decree and declare the blessings of God, the Father, and Jesus Christ His Son over this marriage.

- I decree and declare that the blood of Jesus Christ will cover this marriage and will protect this marriage from all intruders.

- I decree and declare Colossians 2:14 and Galatians 3:13–14 over this marriage.

Having cancelled and blotted out and wiped away the handwriting of the note (bond) with its legal decrees and demands which was in force and stood against us (hostile to us). This [note with its regulations, decrees, and demands] He set aside and cleared completely out of our way by nailing it to [His] cross.

—COLOSSIANS 2:14

Christ purchased our freedom [redeeming us] from the curse (doom) of the Law [and its condemnation] by [Himself] becoming a curse for us, for it is written [in the Scriptures], Cursed is everyone who hangs on a tree (is crucified); to the end that through [their receiving] Christ Jesus, the blessing [promised] to Abraham might come upon the Gentiles, so that we through faith might [all] receive [the realization of] the promise of the [Holy] Spirit.

—GALATIANS 3:13–14

- Based upon this Word of God, I decree and declare in the name of Jesus that no antimarriage forces will come against this marriage and that the Holy Ghost fire with be a hedge of protection around this union.

- I decree and declare that this union is loose from every negative power, generation curse, covenants signed and unsigned, and soul ties from previous relationships in the name of Jesus

- I decree and declare that the man is made in the image and likeness of God and will come into and walk in his God-ordained place as priest, provider, protector, security, and head of this home.

- I decree and declare that this home will be established and governed by the laws of the kingdom of God.

- I decree and declare that their lives together will be soaked in the blood of Jesus Christ.

- I decree and command the spirit of repentance toward God and His Son Jesus Christ to come upon the spirit of rebellion in this household in the name of Jesus.

- I decree and declare that every satanic attack against this marriage will be broken by the blood of Jesus.

- I decree and declare every doorway that is opened to the enemy will be shut to all intruders and that the blood of Jesus will cover this marriage, the home, the children, their finances, and their future.

- I decree and declare that Jesus Christ will be glorified in this home, and the will of God shall be done on the earth as God has decreed it in heaven.

- I come against the spirit of confusion in the midst of this man and his wife projected by any stranger, in-laws or strange spirit in the name of Jesus.

- I decree and declare by the power in the blood of God that this union will be established in the peace, love, and joy of the Holy Ghost.

- I decree and declare God's kingdom shall come into this union in the name of Jesus.

- I decree and declare that God's love will be the shield, the stay, and the foundation of this union in joy or sorrow. When joy comes may we share it together. When sorrow threatens, may we bear it together in gladness or in tears, in sunshine or shadow, and may we ever draw closer to each other and nearer to you, O Lord.

- I decree patience, gentleness, forbearance, understanding, and God's protection for this home from those forces that would break it apart.

- I decree and declare health, long life, and the fulfillment of every good dream. May our love continue throughout our lifetime here on Earth and finally blend into life eternal. Through Christ we pray, amen.

DELIVERANCE FROM DEMONS OF SEXUAL PERVERSION

Confession

Father, in the name of Jesus, I confess to You that in the past, through ignorance, curiosity, and willfulness, I have committed immoral acts. I now recognize these acts as sin and confess this sin in my life, claiming Your forgiveness and mercy though the blood of Jesus. I renounce all contacts I have had in the past with these immoral acts, and close the doorway in my life to all these sinful practices and command the related spirits to leave my life in Jesus' name.

Pray against

Lust (all sex spirits that have entered through the eyes, ears, participation, transfer, or by inheritance)

Sexual perversion of all kinds, including oral sex

Filthy conversations

Filthy imaginations

Pornography

Homosexuality

Lesbianism

Anal sex

Bestiality

Sadism

Masochism

Adultery

Incest

Rape

Immorality

Occult sex

Harlotry

Prostitution

Filthy dreams

Sexual fantasies

Frigidity

Lust of the eyes

Lust of the flesh	Incubi
Impotence	Succubi
Lasciviousness	Lewdness
Nudity	Promiscuity
Flirtation	Seduction
Fornication	Sexual flashbacks

I command every perverse spirit to come out of my sex organs, lips, tongue, taste buds, throat, and mind in the name of Jesus. I loose myself from you, in the name of Jesus, and command you to leave me right now in Jesus' name. Amen.

PRAY FOR THOSE DESIRING A MARRIAGE PARTNER

Confession

Now the Lord God said, It is not good (sufficient, satisfactory) that the man should be alone; I will make him a helper meet (suitable, adapted, complementary) for him.

—GENESIS 2:18

He who finds a [true] wife finds a good thing and obtains favor from the Lord.

—PROVERBS 18:22

If you live in Me [abide vitally united to Me] and My words remain in you and continue to live in your hearts, ask whatever you will, and it shall be done for you.

—JOHN 15:7

Lord, I thank You because You care for me and my life is in Your hand.

Lord, open my spiritual eyes and ears to receive divine revelation concerning my life partner.

Let every hindrance to a happy marital life be removed in the name of Jesus.

Lord, show me any hidden faults in me that will cause problems in my marriage in the name of Jesus.

Father, send Your angels to link me up with Your chosen partner for me in the name of Jesus.

I break any antimarriage generational curse backward to twenty generations in the name of Jesus.

I break every curse brought upon me by inherited sexual sins and also by personal sexual sins in the name of Jesus.

Lord, let Your beauty and glory rest upon me in the name of Jesus.

I renounce and break all antimarriage covenants made by me or on my behalf in the name of Jesus.

Lord, reveal to me Your choice for my life in the name of Jesus.

Lord, let my partner and I be a blessing to Your kingdom in the name of Jesus.

Lord, in Jesus name and with the blood of Jesus, I come against all curses and antimarriage decrees made about my life, in the name of Jesus.

Every spiritual force standing in the way of my breakthrough, I plead the blood of Jesus and release the sword of the Lord, in the name of Jesus.

Lord, I ask forgiveness for trespassing and intruding into someone else's territorial boundary and marriage covenant in the name of Jesus.

In the name of Jesus, I stand against and break loose from the power of:

- Ancestral marriage destruction
- Inherited familiar spirits of divorce
- Marriage to the wrong partner
- Poverty in marriage
- Spirits of abortion, fear, and frustration
- The spirit of error and uncertainty
- Blockages standing against manifestation of miracles.

Thank the Lord for your breakthrough in Jesus' name.

Appendix B

CAN YOU TELL IF YOUR MARRIAGE IS IN TROUBLE?

Your relationship is in trouble if your partner discusses all his pertinent business with relatives and friends and keeps you in the dark about everything.

Your relationship is in trouble if you have to call a member of the family or his best friend to find out where your spouse sleeps at night.

Your relationship is in trouble if you do not have your spouse's cell phone number, and he or she is gone all the time.

Your relationship is in trouble when your spouse criticizes everything you do or don't do and is talking negatively about you with friends, family members, and even strangers. That means your spouse is looking for a way of escape out of the relationship and wants to put the blame for his infidelity on you.

Your relationship is in trouble when your spouse starts dating his ex-girlfriend or sleeping with the mother of his children.

Your relationship is in trouble when your spouse works all the time and does not bring home any money.

Your relationship is in trouble if your spouse tells you the child she just gave birth to may not be yours.

Your relationship is in trouble if your husband is constantly seeking the company of single women, taking them out to lunch or dinner.

Your relationship is in trouble if your spouse no longer wants to be seen with you. You drive separate cars to the same function. Sleep on separate beds in the same house. You never go anywhere together, and your birthday, anniversary, and all the important dates pass by unnoticed and you haven't had a hug in years.

NOTES

Chapter 3
Defining the Need for Covering
1. Roberts Liardon, *God's Generals* (New Kensington, PA: Whitaker House, 2003), 287.
2. Ibid., 288.
3. Ibid., 288.
4. Ibid., 49.
5. Ibid., 58.
6. *Webster's New World Dictionary*, 2nd College Edition (New York: Simon & Schuster, 1982), s.v. "respect."

Chapter 5
Divorce and Remarriage
1. *Webster's New World Dictionary*, s.v. "yoke."
2. David Field, *Family Personalities* (Eugene, OR: Harvest House Publishers, 1988).

Chapter 6
How to Become Single After Divorce
1. *Vine's Expository Dictionary of Old and New Testament Words* (Old Tappan, NJ: Fleming H. Revell, 1971), 311.
2. Ibid.
3. *Webster's New World Dictionary*, s.v. "fallow."
4. Ibid., s.v. "debtor."
5. Don Fleming, *World's Bible Dictionary* (Iowa Falls, IA: World Bible Publishers, n.d.), 401.
6. *Vine's Expository Dictionary*, s.v. "ten."
7. *Webster's New World Dictionary*, s.v. "preparation."

To Contact the Author

eldergemma@msn.com

Web site: www.HarborlightsAsc.org